CLASSICAL COMICS
TEACHING RESOURCE PACK

Making Shakespeare accessible
for teachers and students

Suitable for teaching ages 10–17

Written by: Kornel Kossuth

William Shakespeare

CLASSICAL COMICS
TEACHING RESOURCE PACK
The Tempest

First UK Edition

Published by: Classical Comics Ltd

Written by: Kornel Kossuth

Pencils: Jon Haward
Inks: Gary Erskine
Colours: Nigel Dobbyn
Design & Layout: Jo Wheeler & Carl Andrews

Editor in Chief: Clive Bryant

The rights of Kornel Kossuth, Jon Haward, Gary Erskine and
Nigel Dobbyn to be identified as the artists of this work have
been asserted in accordance with the Copyright, Designs and
Patents Act 1988 sections 77 and 78.

All enquiries should be addressed to:
Classical Comics Ltd.
PO Box 7280
Litchborough
Towcester
NN12 9AR, UK
Tel: 0845 812 3000

education@classicalcomics.com
www.classicalcomics.com

ISBN: 978-1-906332-40-2

Printed in the UK

CONTENTS

INTRODUCTION

WELCOME TO *THE TEMPEST* TEACHING RESOURCE FROM CLASSICAL COMICS.

This resource has manifold aims, which I hope it, much like Ariel, can carry out diligently:

- It is designed to be easy to use, giving teachers who have never worked with *The Tempest* an in-depth guide on a range of activities they can deploy. The approach is therefore comprehensive, and this resource gives you a set of ready-to-teach lessons that need little preparation.

- The division of activities into chapters allows teachers more familiar with the text and its teaching to pick and choose the activities they want. A brief introduction to each topic, designed to kick-start thoughts on the theme, helps teachers re-cap their knowledge.

- Most importantly, this resource aims to provide a variety of activities that stimulate learning and are fun for pupils aged 10-17. Each topic contains a list of lesson ideas followed by photocopiable worksheets for some of the tasks mentioned. For those tasks that involve a more closed response, teacher answer sheets are provided at the back of the book. Of course, the answers provided are mostly suggestions only and by no means exhaustive. Where there is no teacher sheet, the task is designed to be more exploratory, with the emphasis on pupils being able to explain their findings rather than guessing what the pre-fabricated "right" answer might be.

Although designed with the Classical Comics version of *The Tempest* in mind, this resource can be used successfully with the traditional text.

If you would like to send feedback or suggest ways to improve this book, please email education@classicalcomics.com Your thoughts and input are always appreciated.

Kornel Kossuth

"Please you draw near."

THE HISTORICAL BACKGROUND OF *THE TEMPEST*

Introduction

Although any play by Shakespeare can stand alone, a look at the background of the play and the era in which it was written can be helpful to decode the main preoccupations of the work (or the playwright). In this context, a look at Shakespeare's life (what little is known about it) and what was happening at the time can yield interesting results.

The Tempest is of particular interest, as its plot is not based on any one definite source (unlike Shakespeare's other plays). From this, we can assume that the play is concerned with matters that affected, troubled, or interested him.

There are a number of ways pupils can engage with the life and times of Shakespeare and the background of *The Tempest*:

- Pupils can be asked to write an essay on the social and political events that influenced *The Tempest*. This essay would be based on research of one of the three main issues (witchcraft, succession, discovery/colonisation), relating this to the play, and then using the framework contained in the chapter on Themes to plan the essay in more detail.

- Some critics have argued that the epilogue was not written by Shakespeare, but was added later. What, in Shakespeare's life or in the events around the time of its writing, suggest that the epilogue was written by the Bard himself? This could be set up as a formal debate, with two to three speakers making points for one side, and the same amount of pupils speaking for the opposition.

- Pupils (possibly in an interdisciplinary project with Art) can be asked to design their own Shakespeare timeline, making it graphically appealing, but clear. They should also include some other facts from Shakespeare's time that they deem important.

Of course, any work done on the play's background should, quite generally, influence the pupils' reading of the play.

SHAKESPEARE'S TIMES
THEMES OF THE LATE ELIZABETHAN AND EARLY JACOBEAN ERA

Sources
The Tempest is unusual in the canon of Shakespeare's plays in that its plot is not based on any definite source. Nevertheless, there are two clear sources evident within the play. For the shipwreck and some happenings on the island, Shakespeare drew on William Strachey's *A true reportory of the wracke, and redemption of Sir Thomas Gates Knight; (etc.)*; while Gonzalo's musings on the perfect commonwealth hearken back to Michel de Montaigne's essay *Of the Caniballes*. However, the play as a whole taps into many ideas and concerns that were current at the time of its writing.

Succession
One pressing question for most of the Elizabethan era was that of succession. Elizabeth had a difficult ascent to the throne, having to contend against her first cousin once removed, Mary, Queen of Scots (Mary's son, James VI, became King James I of England after Elizabeth died in 1603). The fact that Elizabeth did not marry and thus was without a legitimate heir caused widespread consternation during her rule; and Shakespeare more than once wrote about the dangers of an uncertain succession and the need for a united England in the 1590s (when Elizabeth was already in her late fifties).

The question of succession had been resolved by the time *The Tempest* was written. Despite that, it remained an issue until the Act of Settlement in 1701; and so concerns over legitimate rulership and their heirs for the realm would have been present in the minds of the public.

It is certain that audiences of the play would have understood this to be one of the major themes. It is also interesting to note that the solution to the issue of Elizabeth's succession was the fusion of two kingdoms: Scotland and England (much like the solution to Prospero's issues of legitimacy is the fusion of Milan and Naples).

Magic and Witchcraft
Although nowadays we have a varied and quite liberal view of magic and have separated it from witchcraft and devil worship, the two were inextricably linked in Shakespeare's day. Anyone capable of magic was thought to be in league with the forces of evil – a concept expounded by *The Malleus Maleficarum*, the ultimate witch-hunter's manual.

King James I had also written a book on witches, his *Daemonologie* (1597), in which he expounded his belief in witches and witchcraft. Indeed, he believed himself to have been at the receiving end of magic: when James returned from Denmark with his new wife, Anne of Denmark, he was caught in a storm, which was believed to have been caused by witches. The suspects were subsequently interrogated, (partly by James himself) tortured, and executed.

In this respect it is interesting – and possibly quite risky of Shakespeare – that the main character is a magician who causes a storm to wreck a ship, a fate James I believed he had escaped. It is hard to imagine the king could have seen any magician as not being in league with Satan.

The way Shakespeare solves this apparent paradox is to have Prospero renounce his magic at the end of the play and go into government as a mundane human being. The epilogue, asking for the audience to pray for him and grant him mercy so that he can leave the island, may also have the double meaning of forgiving Prospero for his sin of witchcraft.

Discoveries and Colonisation
Colonisation is dealt with in greater depth in the section of Themes. However, the Elizabethan era was also one of discoveries and long sea voyages. After the New World was discovered, settlements were established in North America by adventurers like Sir Walter Raleigh; these would later form the first colonies.

It is important to bear in mind that explorers and colonisers like Raleigh were, more or less, a law unto themselves. Backed by their monarch, they were permitted to do anything they decided in order to further their endeavours.

Shakespeare's response to issues of colonisation is not clear, but it is possible to interpret the end of the play as his proposed solution, in which the "Westerners" leave the island, implying that they should leave the New World alone.

Religion
What is startling is that Shakespeare is silent on the issue of religion, even though it was a major factor in the politics of the day. Mary, the predecessor of Queen Elizabeth I, was a Catholic and forced the kingdom (that had only recently adopted a mild form of Protestantism under Henry VIII) to adopt Catholicism. Elizabeth reverted back to Protestantism, and Catholics were persecuted in her reign and under James I, too, especially after the failed Gunpowder Plot. But various Protestant factions were also pushing for a bishop-less church and a clearer break with Rome. The monarchy eventually settled for a bishop-led Church of England, but the ongoing religious tensions led to the first religiously-motivated emigrations to North America.

Shakespeare's avoidance of religious issues may be because he thought the subject too contentious – he definitely wouldn't have wanted to upset his king on such a delicate subject. It may also have been that Shakespeare himself was a closet Catholic (like his father apparently was) and wanted to avoid drawing attention to himself. Nevertheless, for someone so in step with his time, it is a strange and notable omission.

EXPLORING ISSUES IN SHAKESPEARE'S TIME
"'Tis far off, and rather like a dream, than an assurance"

Use the following grid to guide your research into themes that were current in Shakespeare's day and how they are mirrored in *The Tempest*.

Issue: _____

Question	In Shakespeare's time?	How is it reflected in the play?
In what way was the issue important?		
What were the various points of view on the issue?		
What solution (if any) was there to the issue?		

SHAKESPEARE TIMELINE

Approx. Dates	Plays	What happened at the time?
1564		William Shakespeare was born in Stratford-upon-Avon, England on 23rd April.
1572		Shakespeare possibly started at the New King's School grammar school in Stratford.
1582		Shakespeare married Ann Hathaway. By 1585 they had 3 children.
1586-1592	Maybe Shakespeare started writing his poems here. No one knows exactly when he wrote them. By 1601 he had written these poems: *Venus and Adonis* *The Rape of Lucrece* *Sonnets* *A Lover's Complaint* *The Phoenix and the Turtle*	Nobody knows! Some people think that he travelled abroad, or that he was a teacher, or that he ran away from Stratford because he was in trouble for stealing a deer! He may have been one of "The Queen's Men" group of actors. In 1592 the playwright Robert Greene called Shakespeare an "upstart crow" – he was jealous of the brilliant new writer!
1593		Shakespeare's friend and fellow playwright Christopher Marlowe was killed in a tavern in Deptford. All the theatres were closed because of the plague.
Before 1594	*Henry VI* (three parts) *Richard III* *Titus Andronicus* *Love's Labour's Lost* *The Two Gentlemen of Verona* *The Comedy of Errors* *The Taming of the Shrew*	Shakespeare joined "The Lord Chamberlain's Men" company of actors when the theatres reopened.
1594-1597	*Romeo and Juliet* *A Midsummer Night's Dream* *Richard II* *King John* *The Merchant of Venice*	About this time, we think that Shakespeare wrote *Love's Labour's Won*, but the play has been lost.
1597-1600	*Henry IV part i* *Henry IV part ii* *Henry V* *Much Ado About Nothing* *Merry Wives of Windsor* *As You Like It* *Julius Caesar* *Troilus and Cressida*	In 1597, Shakespeare bought a house in Stratford. In 1598, The Theatre in London burned down. In 1599, just after he finished *Henry V*, Shakespeare's company had The Theatre rebuilt as The Globe.
1601-1608	*Hamlet* *Twelfth Night* *Measure For Measure* *All's Well That Ends Well* *Othello* *King Lear* *Macbeth* *Timon of Athens* *Antony and Cleopatra* *Coriolanus*	Queen Elizabeth I died in 1603. James VI became James I of England and Wales. King James became the patron of Shakespeare's company, renaming it "The King's Men", giving it royal support. In 1605, Guy Fawkes tried to blow up Parliament.
After 1608	*Pericles* *Cymbeline* *The Winter's Tale* *The Tempest* *Henry VIII*	In 1613, The Globe burned down, then was rebuilt in 1614. Shakespeare retired to Stratford and did some writing with John Fletcher, his successor in "The King's Men". He died in 1616. In 1623, his plays were collected and published in the *First Folio*.

THE GLOBE

GLOBE THEATRE: Label Descriptions

These are all jumbled up. Work out which description goes with which name, then label the diagram of The Globe with the information that you think is correct.

	Name	Description
1		The canopy over the stage, decorated with signs of the zodiac. There was a space above here from which actors could be lowered through a trapdoor as gods or angels.
2		Sometimes live music was played here, but it was also used for acting as a wall or balcony.
3		There were trunks of oak trees put here to hold up The Heavens. The theatre was meant to be like the universe – divided into Heaven, Earth and Hell.
4		A thousand "groundlings" would stand here to watch the plays. Noisy and smelly!
5		Here was the best place to sit if you were a lord or lady because everyone could see you – but your view might not be very good!
6		This led down to Hell! It was a room below the stage from where actors playing ghosts, witches and devils could make their entrance.
7		Rich playgoers could sit here on cushioned seats.
8		An area behind the stage where costumes and props were kept and where actors changed.

Name	Number of description
The Heavens	
The Gentlemen's Rooms	
The Trapdoor	
The Yard	
The Musician's Gallery	
The Lord's Rooms	
The Tiring House	
The Pillars	

THE GLOBE

GLOBE THEATRE: Label Descriptions
Fill in the labels using the descriptions provided.

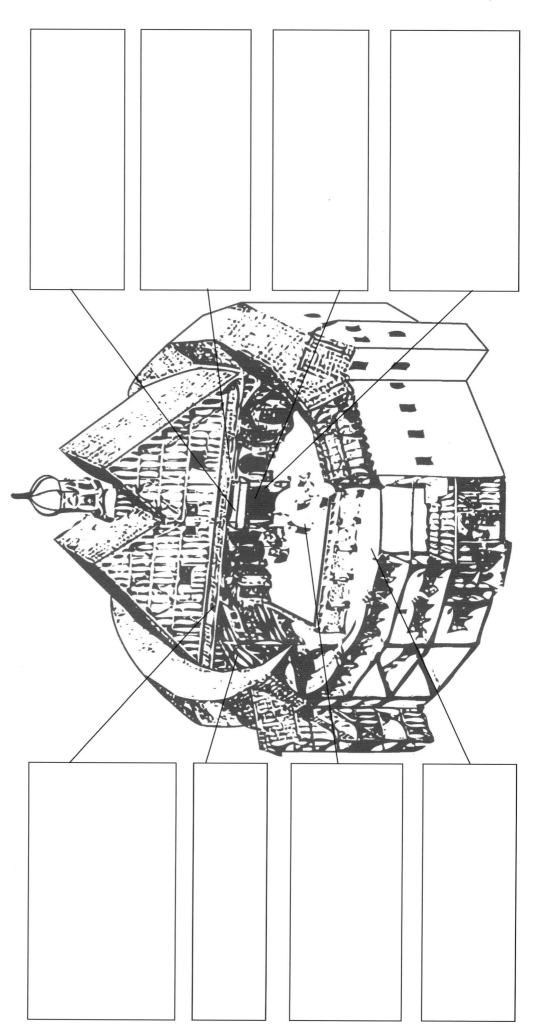

SCENE-BY-SCENE SYNOPSIS

Act I Scene I

The ship's Master and Boatswain are trying to guide their ship through a heavy storm. King Alonso, Antonio and Gonzalo (the king's advisor) appear on the deck, where they are rudely rebuked that they are in the way and sent back down to their cabins. A short time later, Sebastian (the king's brother), Antonio and Gonzalo appear again. The Boatswain again chides them. The ship breaks; Sebastian and Antonio blame the Boatswain. Every man tries to save himself.

Act I Scene II

Miranda begs her father, Prospero, if he is the origin of the storm, to abate it and spare the lives of those involved. Prospero assures her that no one has come to any harm.

Prospero then tells Miranda about his (and her) past: twelve years ago, Prospero was Duke of Milan. Preferring his studies of arcane arts to government, Prospero left the running of the state to his brother, Antonio. Antonio advanced his henchmen and subsequently ousted his brother from the Dukedom with the help of Alonso, the King of Naples; in return, Antonio swore allegiance to Naples. Rather than being put to death, Prospero was set adrift in a small boat with Miranda. Gonzalo, appointed with despatching Prospero, provided him with food, clothes and his magic books. By chance, the two exiles reached the island. Now chance has brought Prospero's enemies within his reach, so he conjured the storm to bring them onto the island and into his power. At the end of his narrative, Prospero uses a spell to send Miranda to sleep. Prospero calls on Ariel, his servant spirit, and asks him if he has obeyed Prospero's orders regarding the storm. Ariel reports that no one is harmed; that he left Ferdinand, Alonso's son, alone; that the ship was safe in a bay, with all the mariners locked inside; and that the rest of Alonso's fleet was on its way to Naples, believing the king drowned. Ariel seeks his freedom from Prospero's service. Prospero reminds Ariel that he saved Ariel from his twelve-year imprisonment in a split pine tree – where the evil witch Sycorax had bound him because of his refusal to carry out her demands. Prospero promises to release Ariel in two days' time, if he does Prospero's bidding. Ariel flies off, invisible, to carry out Prospero's orders. Prospero wakes Miranda, and together they go to Caliban, the semi-human son of Sycorax. Caliban complains about his treatment from Prospero. He claims the island as his, because his mother Sycorax, when she was exiled from Algiers, took possession of it. When Prospero first landed, he feigned kindness towards Caliban, so the latter showed him round the island. Prospero refutes Caliban's claim and contends that Miranda and he treated him kindly and educated him until he tried to rape Miranda. Prospero commands Caliban to fetch wood, and, fearful of his magical powers, Caliban agrees.

Ariel draws Ferdinand towards Prospero and Miranda. When they see each other, Miranda and Ferdinand are both equally struck by the other's appearance, and Ferdinand, thinking he is the sole survivor of the shipwreck, proposes to make Miranda his bride. Prospero acts in a hostile manner towards Ferdinand and accuses of him of spying. He casts a spell on Ferdinand and, despite Miranda's intercessions on his behalf, leads him away as a captive.

SCENE-BY-SCENE SYNOPSIS

Act II Scene I

Gonzalo tries to cheer Alonso up over the loss of his son, contending they at least have their lives. Sebastian and Antonio mock Gonzalo. Their perception of the island seems to differ, too: while Gonzalo sees a verdant island and their clothes freshly washed, Antonio and Sebastian see a barren land and their clothes unchanged. Alonso mourns the loss of both his children: his daughter Claribel to the King of Tunis in marriage and his son Ferdinand in the shipwreck, both of which Sebastian (Alonso's brother) blames on Alonso. Gonzalo explains what he would do, were he king of the island. Ariel enters and uses magic to send everyone except Antonio and Sebastian to sleep. With reference to how he gained the Dukedom of Milan from his own brother (Prospero), Antonio explains to Sebastian that, because Ferdinand is dead (or so they think) and Claribel is far away, Sebastian would become King of Naples if Alonso and Gonzalo were to die. As the two are about to kill Alonso and Gonzalo, Ariel wakes the latter, who wakes his king. They are both surprised to see Antonio and Sebastian with drawn swords and without convincing excuses as to why. Alonso leads the courtiers off in search of his son.

Act II Scene II

Caliban is scared of Prospero punishing him for working too slowly. As Trinculo (a jester to King Alonso) approaches, Caliban thinks he is one of Prospero's agents and hides himself underneath his cloak. Trinculo wonders at the strange apparition of Caliban, before he too hides under Caliban's cloak, to escape the approaching storm. Stephano (a butler to the King) wanders along (drunk!) and marvels at this strange two-headed beast that talks (which, of course, is just Caliban and Trinculo hiding under the same cloak). He gives Caliban's half of the "monster" some of his alcohol. Trinculo makes himself known to his drinking companion. Under the influence of the alcohol, Caliban swears to serve Stephano and promises to show him all the sweet spots of the island. As Stephano and Trinculo believe they are the sole survivors, Stephano decides to take control of the island as its king. Caliban is elated to have gained freedom from Prospero as Stephano's servant.

Act III Scene I

Although Ferdinand is made to carry logs by Prospero, he delights in the work as long as it means being close to Miranda. Miranda even offers to help Ferdinand carry the wood, but he refuses. They declare their love for one another and are subsequently engaged. Prospero, who watches the encounter in secret, is pleased with the outcome.

Act III Scene II

Caliban, ever fawning on Stephano, sows dissent between his new-found master and Trinculo. Ariel adds to the confusion by emulating Trinculo's voice and accusing Caliban of lying when he tells of how he was enslaved by Prospero. Caliban incites Stephano to try to kill Prospero while he takes his afternoon nap. Stephano looks forward to kingship on the island with Miranda as his wife and Caliban and Trinculo his viceroys. Ariel, who has overhead the plot, leaves to tell Prospero. Ariel returns to lure the plotters away with his music.

Act III Scene III

King Alonso and his courtiers are weary from their search for Ferdinand. Unseen by them, Prospero conjures up strange creatures that bring in a feast. They marvel at the sight, and although they are wary, they decide to eat, as they are hungry. Just as Alonso is about to start, the food disappears, and Ariel, in the guise of a harpy, berates the "three men of sin" and tells Alonso that he lost his son as punishment for the ousting of Prospero from Milan. Not sure they can believe their own eyes, Alonso is struck by Ariel's speech and filled with remorse. Antonio and Sebastian, however, are only intent on catching and silencing whoever spoke.

SCENE-BY-SCENE SYNOPSIS

Act IV Scene I

Prospero admits to having tested Ferdinand to be sure of his intentions and gives him Miranda in marriage. He insists that the two remain chaste until the wedding. Prospero despatches Ariel to fetch the others while he entertains Miranda and Prospero with a masque. In the masque, the goddesses Iris, Ceres and Juno praise conjugal love and bless the two young lovers. Prospero abruptly ends the masque when he remembers that Caliban and Stephano plan to kill him. He tries to put Ferdinand and Miranda at ease that he is all right and calls Ariel. Ariel reports that he led the three drunkards through thorn bushes and into a smelly bog. Prospero orders Ariel to prepare a further trap of fine clothes for the three and vows to make them pay for their presumptuousness.

In low spirits, Stephano, Trinculo and Caliban arrive at Prospero's cell. There, they discover the fine clothing, which Stephano and Trinculo try on – despite Caliban's exhortation to leave the clothes and kill Prospero. Prospero and Ariel set spirits in the guise of hunting dogs on them to chase them away.

Act V Scene I

Prospero and Ariel, whom Prospero has promised soon to set free, review the afternoon's work. Ariel reports that Alonso and the courtiers are all close by and in such a state that even he, a spirit, would pity them. Prospero decides not to exact revenge on them. While Ariel fetches the courtiers, Prospero conjures one final spell before renouncing his magic. The men stand charmed in a circle and slowly come to their senses as Prospero speaks and forgives them for their various wrongdoings. With Ariel's help, Prospero clothes himself as he was when Duke of Milan. The courtiers are not sure whether to believe their eyes. Alonso is interested in the particulars of Prospero's survival, while Antonio and Sebastian seem unrepentant. The courtiers discover Ferdinand and Miranda playing chess – and Alonso, delighted to see his son alive and well again, gives his consent for the two to be married. Gonzalo is ecstatic at the fortunate turn of events. Ariel leads the ship's Master and Boatswain, unscathed, to the group. Ariel then drives in Caliban, Stephano and Trinculo, still dressed in the clothes they stole. Prospero assumes responsibility for a seemingly reformed Caliban. Prospero invites the courtiers to stay the night in his cell and listen to his story before returning to Italy the next day. With the charge to provide favourable winds for their return journey, Prospero releases Ariel.

Epilogue

Without his magic, Prospero turns to the audience and asks for applause – because only that can set him truly free from his island captivity.

COMPREHENSION

ACT I

Fill in the blanks using the words provided. You may use a word once only, and you may not need to use all of them.

On returning home from _____, the King of Naples and his courtiers are caught in a _____ close to an _____. The ship _____, and all seems lost.

On the island, Miranda begs her _____, _____, to make sure that no one is hurt in the storm. Prospero reassures her and tells her about their past: _____ years ago, Prospero was Duke of _____. He allowed his _____, _____, to govern instead of him, as he preferred to spend his time in _____. Eventually, with the help of Alonso, the King of _____, Antonio deposed his brother and set him, together with _____, adrift in a small boat. They reached the island onto which Antonio, Alonso and the royal _____ are now wrecked. Having put Miranda to sleep, Prospero calls on Ariel, his servant _____. Ariel wants his freedom, but Prospero reminds him how indebted he is to Prospero for rescuing him from a _____. Ariel flies off to carry out Prospero's orders, while the latter wakes Miranda.

Prospero and Miranda visit Caliban, a _____ servant, whom Prospero claims he treated kindly until Caliban tried to _____ Miranda. Caliban is sent off to fetch wood.

Ariel brings Ferdinand, the son of _____, to Prospero and Miranda. The two young people _____ at first sight, but Prospero takes Ferdinand _____, claiming he is a _____.

twelve   entourage   party   brutish

tempest   spy   island   Miranda

Prospero   Alonso   father   uncle   Milan

hounds   Antonio   kill   fall in love

Duke   Naples   Gonzalo   brother   rape

study   Tunis   Sebastian   hate each

other   breaks   pine tree   prisoner

spirit

16

COMPREHENSION

ACT II

Alonso is distraught over the loss of his _____ and _____, _____. Nothing _____ says can cheer him up, not even his musings about what he would do, were he _____ of the island. Alonso feels he has lost his _____, too, as she has just been married to the King of Tunis. Typically (and very unsympathetically) _____ says Alonso only has _____ to blame for that.

_____ casts a sleep spell over the courtiers, with the exception of Antonio and Sebastian. Antonio suggests to Sebastian that they kill _____ and Gonzalo, which would make Sebastian King of Naples, in much the same way that _____ became Duke of Milan. Just as the two are about to strike, Ariel wakes Gonzalo, who in turn wakes the king. The two plotters make up a swift _____ about why their swords are drawn, and they all leave to go in search of Ferdinand.

Elsewhere on the island, Caliban is fetching wood for Prospero. Caliban is scared of his master and hides underneath his _____ when he sees what he believes to be a _____ approaching. It is _____, who takes refuge under the same gabardine to escape the approaching _____. When _____ arrives, he is amazed to see the strange _____ with four legs and two heads. He gives the monster drink, and Trinculo, realising that it is Stephano, greets his friend. _____ promises to be a loyal servant to Stephano.

Miranda   **barrel**   **king**   **excuse**   **storm**   **Sebastian**   **Alonso**   **brother**   **Caliban**   **heir**

Stephano   **Antonio**   **Trinculo**   **lie**   **duke**   **the wreck**   **Ferdinand**   **himself**   **creature**   **cloak**

Gonzalo   **Ariel**   **Prospero**   **son**   **poem**   **daughter**   **the voyage**   **spirit**   **magic**   **rapier**

ACT III

Ferdinand has to do work for _____, but he is happy to do it as long as it allows him to be close to _____. They decide to _____, which pleases Prospero, who has been _____ on their conversation. Ariel goes to Stephano, Trinculo and Caliban, and copies _____'s voice, thus sowing discord among the three drunkards. Caliban tells _____ of how Prospero made him his slave and persuades Stephano to kill Prospero in order to become king of the island, taking Miranda as his _____. Ariel overhears the murderous plot and rushes off to tell Prospero.

Alonso and the _____ are tired from searching for _____. Exhausted, they see _____ laying out a feast. They are _____, and they decide to _____. However, it is Prospero who conjured up the feast, and just as _____ approaches the food, it disappears. _____ reappears, transformed into a frightening _____. In this guise, he tells Alonso that Ferdinand was _____ as punishment to Alonso for him helping to _____ Prospero. The king is filled with remorse, but _____ and Sebastian are _____.

Ariel   **kill**   **a mermaid**   **marry**   **Stephano**   **Miranda**   **Sebastian**   **Trinculo**   **Caliban**

spirits   **courtiers**   **famished**   **drowned**   **rescue**   **Alonso**   **depose**   **servant**   **unrepentant**

wife   **in love**   **eavesdropping**   **watching**   **Antonio**   **Ferdinand**   **starve**   **mariners**   **harpy**

Prospero   **alive**   **eat**

COMPREHENSION

ACT IV

Having tested Ferdinand's love, Prospero agrees to let him _____ Miranda. He makes _____ promise not to _____ with Miranda until their wedding night. To celebrate their impending _____, Prospero has _____ perform a masque, in which _____ goddesses _____ marital love and chastity, and bless the happy couple. The masque ends suddenly when _____ remembers _____'s plot to _____ him.

_____ reports that he has led the three plotters astray and left them in a smelly _____. Prospero prepares a further _____. Arriving at Prospero's _____, Stephano, Trinculo and Caliban are despondent. They discover some fancy _____, and _____ and Trinculo try them on. Caliban tries to remind them of their purpose, but his words are in vain. Prospero conjures up some spirits as _____ to chase and _____ all three of them.

praise   Caliban   cell   bog   murder   Stephano   true   Sebastian   Ferdinand   Greek Norse   clothes   wedding   kiss   palace   sleep   goblins   entertainment   hunting dogs insignia   punish   actors   Ariel   kill   spirits   Prospero   Miranda   fire   marry   trap

ACT V

Prospero promises Ariel that he will soon be free. _____ reports the events of the _____. He has managed to bring all _____ near to Prospero's cell. Ariel encourages Prospero to _____ his brother and _____. The courtiers arrive at the _____, and Prospero charms them all. He _____ each one separately, then puts on the _____ he wore when he was Duke of Milan. All are _____ to see him again. Alonso wonders how he managed to arrive on _____, but Antonio and _____ still do not seem to _____. Prospero reveals Ferdinand and Miranda to Alonso and the courtiers. Overjoyed to see his son alive, Alonso agrees to their being _____. Ariel now brings the ship's Master and _____ to the cell, unharmed. Caliban, _____ and Trinculo are also driven in by Ariel and, while Alonso recognises Stephano and _____, Prospero takes the responsibility for _____, who appears to have seen the error of his ways. Prospero _____ Ariel, asking him only to provide fair _____ for their return journey to _____. In the epilogue, Prospero turns to the _____ and asks them to set him free with their _____.

his magic   applause   Stephano   clothes   repent   Gonzalo   afternoon   care   releases Italy   Sebastian   Tunis   Alonso   the   island   parties   hate   Boatswain   murder Caliban   courtiers   forgive   forgives   cell   Ariel   invokes   winds   Trinculo   married audience   surprised

WHAT HAPPENS NEXT?

TASK:

Look closely at the pictures on each card in the following pages. In the box, write down what you think is happening in each scene. You need to know the play first!

Comic Card	WHAT IS HAPPENING? Describe in your own words. Try to explain what is going on in each panel and what characters are saying. Can you remember what happens next?
Card 1	
Card 2	
Card 3	
Card 4	

COMIC CARD 1
The Tempest Act I Scene II

COMIC CARD 2

The Tempest Act II Scene I

COMIC CARD 3
The Tempest Act II Scene II

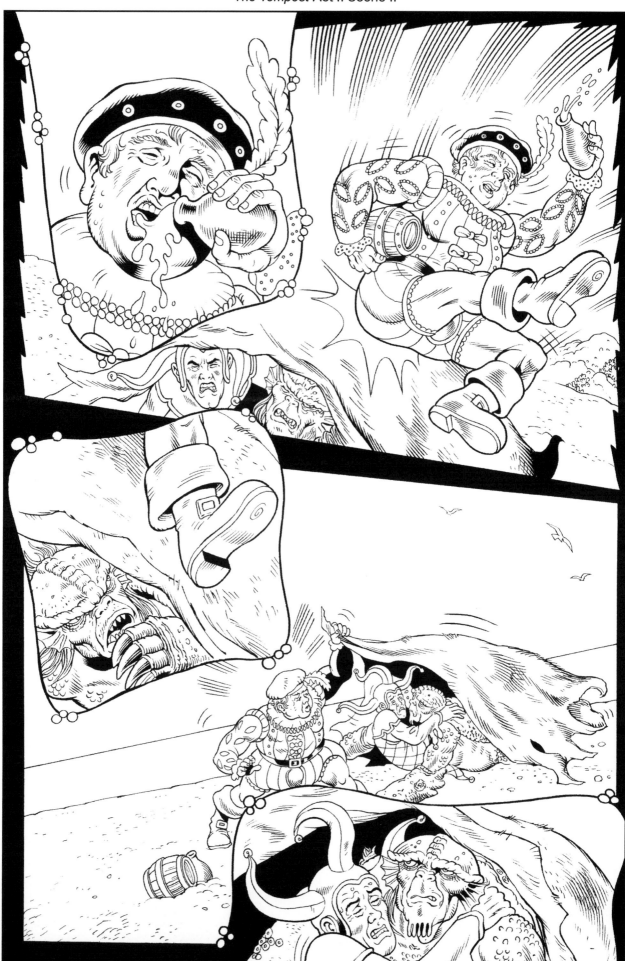

COMIC CARD 4

The Tempest Act V Scene I

THE ENDING OF *THE TEMPEST*

"To prayers, to prayers! All lost!"

In a number of plays, mostly the comedies, Shakespeare adds an epilogue at the end of the action. The epilogue is usually delivered by one of the characters, and its purpose is to apologise for the insufficiencies of the play and seek the audience's goodwill and approval through its applause. As such, it is quite a stock piece. However, Shakespeare manages to provide interesting variations on this theme, none more so than in *The Tempest*, where the epilogue has also been seen as his farewell to the stage. Because the ending of *The Tempest* has drawn so much critical attention, it is worth examining its difference from the epilogues of other plays.

TASK:

With the aid of the following extracts from other Shakespeare plays and the comparison chart, compare and contrast the epilogue from *The Tempest* with one or more of the others.

From *A Midsummer Night's Dream*

PUCK
If we shadows have offended,
Think but this, and all is mended,
That you have but slumber'd here
While these visions did appear.
And this weak and idle theme,
No more yielding but a dream,
Gentles, do not reprehend:
If you pardon, we will mend.
And, as I am an honest Puck,
If we have unearned luck
Now to 'scape the serpent's tongue,
We will make amends ere long:
Else the Puck a liar call.
So, good night unto you all.
Give me your hands, if we be friends,
And Robin shall restore amends.

From *All's Well That Ends Well*

KING
The king's a beggar now the play is done.
All is well ended, if this suit be won,
That you express content; which we will pay,
With strife to please you, day exceeding day:
Ours be your patience then, and yours our parts;
Your gentle hands lend us, and take our hearts.

From *As You Like It*

ROSALIND
It is not the fashion to see the lady the epilogue; but it is no more unhandsome, than to see the lord the prologue. If it be true that good wine needs no bush, 'tis true that a good play needs no epilogue; yet to good wine they do use good bushes, and good plays prove the better by the help of good epilogues. What a case am I in then, that am neither a good epilogue, nor cannot insinuate with you in the behalf of a good play? I am not furnished like a beggar, therefore to beg will not become me: my way is to conjure you; and I'll begin with the women. I charge you, O women! for the love you bear to men, to like as much of this play as please you: and I charge you, O men! for the love you bear to women -- as I perceive by your simpering, none of you hates them -- that between you and the women, the play may please. If I were a woman, I would kiss as many of you as had beards that pleased me, complexions that liked me and breaths that I defied not: and, I am sure, as many as have good beards, or good faces, or sweet breaths, will, for my kind offer, when I make curtsy, bid me farewell.

THE ENDING OF *THE TEMPEST*

Comparison Chart

	The Tempest		
Who delivers the epilogue?			
Is the actor still speaking "in character"?			
How is the speaker trying to persuade the audience to clap?			
How do you think the speech would be delivered – and what does that tell you about the character?			

EXPLORING CHARACTER

Introduction

This chapter looks at the characters in *The Tempest*. The play poses quite a challenge to character studies as it is unduly weighted towards one character only, namely Prospero. He speaks 674 lines, as opposed to 194 lines by the next-closest character, Ariel, and 175 by Caliban.

The main brunt of character work will therefore focus on Prospero and his two servants Ariel and Caliban. Prospero, often likened to Shakespeare and seen as his imago, is multi-faceted: harsh, yet forgiving, exacting, yet benevolent. After Prospero, Caliban has possibly attracted the most varied responses: from dull animalistic semi-human savage to misunderstood and exploited native.

However, many other characters are worthy of deeper exploration: Antonio and Sebastian, for example, are interesting as prototypes of evil, scheming and ambitious courtiers, although a closer look will reveal that Sebastian may not be quite as dastardly as a cursory reading may suggest. The relationship between Stephano and Trinculo changes as a result of Caliban's influence, making it worthwhile to explore the subtle differences between Act II Sc II and Act III Sc II.

The dearth of lines for most characters can also be seen as an advantage, leading to great freedom and creativity in fleshing out the characters from the little we know of them. Francisco, for example, only speaks 11 lines but is on stage a great deal. What does he do during this time? This ultimately leads to the question of what kind of a character he is. As can be seen, much character-related work is connected to drama activities, stagecraft and thematical work.

THE MAIN CHARACTERS

Prospero

Prospero is the central and dominant figure of *The Tempest*. He is both a nobleman and a magician and thus straddles two worlds: the real world of courtly politics and the fantasy world of spirits and magic. It seems Prospero was once more interested in the fantasy world, neglecting his role as ruler of Milan, but the play shows him devising his return to power and discarding his magic, settling for one world only in the end.

The plot of the play is driven by Prospero's desire for revenge, but ultimately he does not take his vengeance, prompted by Ariel to forgive the perpetrators. Even though the entire play is controlled by Prospero, he has traditionally been portrayed as benevolent, gently pushing the characters in the right direction. However, modern interpretations often highlight the more troubled side of Prospero: his need to control everything and everyone and his harsh, almost cruel, treatment of Caliban.

In the play, Prospero has a number of functions, each reflecting on his personality: magician and student of occult art, worldly ruler, father, revenger, mortal human being, lord and master (to his servants), theatre-manager – and maybe even Shakespeare himself!

Ariel

Most of Prospero's magic seems to be channelled through or actually done by Ariel, his airy spirit. Associated with air, Ariel is obviously to be thought of as a light and lithe spirit, possibly like the wind or the sun. He can change shape at will, appearing in various guises throughout the play.

Although referred to as "he" in the play (a denomination kept in this resource), Ariel's gender (being a spirit) is uncertain, and in the past he has been played by both male and female actors, also to highlight issues of gender and control.

Just as the play from Prospero's point of view is about vengeance, for Ariel it is about gaining his freedom. This seems to depend on him carrying out Prospero's work to the best of his abilities, which he does. Act I Scene II contains a hint of rebelliousness in Ariel, which can be expanded upon, although the further interchanges do not seem to suggest a tense relationship between Prospero and Ariel – indeed, Ariel is prime informer and executor for Prospero, acting like his right-hand man.

EXPLORING CHARACTER

Caliban

Described as "a savage and deformed slave", Caliban is the one character that has undergone the most revision through time. Seen originally as a brute providing comic relief, most productions now take a more varied and subtle approach to his character.

Caliban bears a grudge against Prospero because the latter robbed him of what Caliban sees as his island (Sycorax was pregnant with Caliban when she arrived on the island. Because he was born there, is he also an immigrant?). Caliban is powerless against Prospero's magic, and so his aggression manifests itself in curses, reluctance and subterfuges. His attempt to rape Miranda and his inciting of Stephano and Trinculo to kill Prospero are both indirect attacks against his master. He also shows himself to be a perfect boot-licker, once again using his cunning, this time to play Trinculo off against Stephano.

Of course, it can be said that all these actions are the result of his oppression, which makes it impossible for him to express himself freely. Seen like this, Caliban becomes a more tragic figure who is prevented by Prospero from fulfilling his potential and taking on his birthright (just like Prospero was ousted by Antonio). So, perhaps, Caliban and Prospero are similar after all and what repulses Prospero about Caliban is what he sees of himself in the monster.

Miranda

Miranda seems to be almost ethereal and not of this world. Both Ferdinand and Alonso believe her to be a goddess when they first see her. She seems to be all innocence and goodness, to the point of being naïve. She is, therefore, much like a fairy-tale princess. True to type, she has led a cloistered existence so far, Prospero being her only mentor and contact, except for Caliban, who tried to rape her. Her knowledge of the world is thus limited.

Nevertheless, she is not quite as straightforward as she sounds. She hurls abuse at Caliban (in a speech often attributed to Prospero due to its unseemliness for a female) and defies her father by meeting with Ferdinand, telling him her name and vowing to marry him.

Antonio and Sebastian

The true "men of sin" seem to be very similar. Although they are alike in many respects, Antonio is the active principle, pursuing his ambition and taking action to achieve his (evil) ends. Sebastian, on the other hand, is passive, not acting of his own accord, and only at the instigation of others. Nevertheless, Sebastian is open to Antonio's ideas and, once convinced, pursues his ends, too.

All through Prospero's efforts to purge Alonso, Antonio and Sebastian of sin, these two remain unaffected and unrepentant. They end the play in the same mocking, life-denying tone in which they made their first appearance. For them, nothing has changed, and one can only wonder what they will do in the future.

Stephano and Trinculo

These two are almost the comic counterparts of Antonio and Sebastian, their outlook on life being very similar (if somewhat baser), as evidenced by their reaction to Caliban. However, they are also an unequal pair: it seems that Trinculo, the jester, has more of a sense of reality than Stephano, who is completely taken in by Caliban and lets greed and violence get the better of him. That said, Trinculo is too cowardly to defend himself or to act according to his (slightly better) judgment.

FAMILY TREE

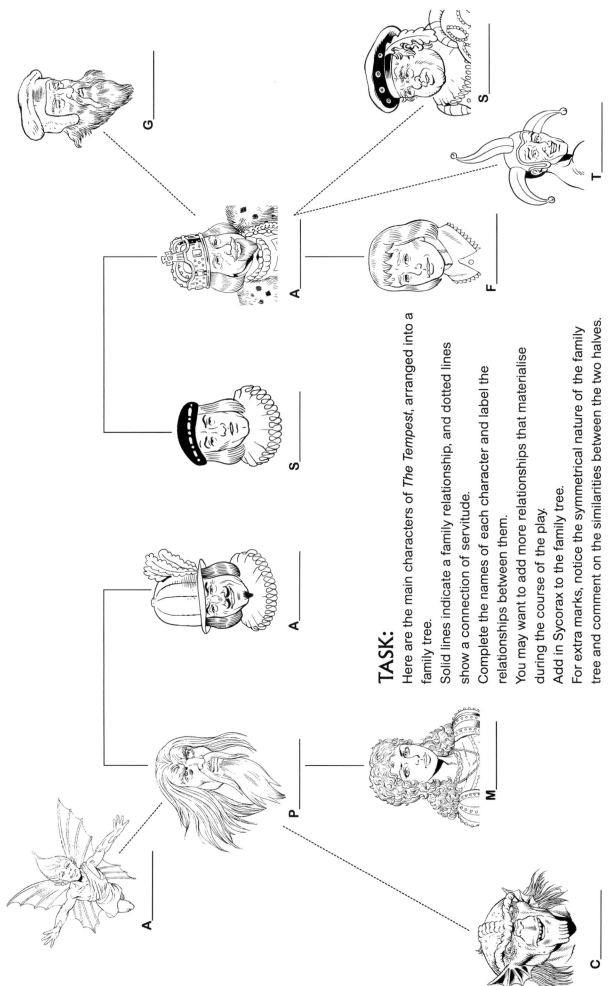

TASK:

Here are the main characters of *The Tempest*, arranged into a family tree.

Solid lines indicate a family relationship, and dotted lines show a connection of servitude.

Complete the names of each character and label the relationships between them.

You may want to add more relationships that materialise during the course of the play.

Add in Sycorax to the family tree.

For extra marks, notice the symmetrical nature of the family tree and comment on the similarities between the two halves.

EXPLORING CHARACTER - ACTIVITIES

PROSPERO'S RELATIONSHIPS IN ACT I, SCENE II:

One important way to discover someone's character is to see how he or she reacts to other people: how do they respond to the lines of other characters?

Prospero is undoubtedly the central character of *The Tempest* – all other characters revolve around him. It is therefore important in the scheme of the play to clarify the relationship between Prospero and the other characters, at the same time clarifying their personalities early in the story. This is the purpose of Act I Sc II. In this scene, Prospero interacts and has lengthy dialogues with Miranda, Ariel, Caliban and Ferdinand.

There are a number of ways to analyse character and relationships in Act I Sc II. To aid with the exploration of character and relationships, this resource provides a relationship chart and extracts from the play with questions in the right-hand margin.

Here are some task ideas:

- Split the class into groups and assign a character to each group. Using evidence from the text, the group must analyse what kind of a person that character is. The findings should be recorded (using bullet points) and then shared with the other groups.

- Split the class into groups and assign a relationship between two characters to each group. The group must go through the text and record its findings, possibly in note form, on the relationship chart (which can be updated as pupils work through the play). The group can also deduce character traits from the relationship. Once again, the findings should be shared so each pupil can complete the relationship chart.

- For a more structured and supported analysis of Act I Sc II, groups of pupils can be given the text extracts reprinted here and asked to analyse relationship and character based on the questions posed in the right-hand margin. Findings can then be shared, and you may decide to also record them in the relationship chart.

TEXT WORK:

Here are some further ideas for character and relationship analysis:

- Act II Sc I: Here we see the courtiers on the island for the first time after the storm. They each react differently to their surroundings. It is a good idea to focus on Antonio and Sebastian in this scene, particularly on their plot to kill Alonso and Gonzalo, as this portrays the two villains most closely and highlights the differences between them. Working in pairs, one pupil should concentrate on Antonio, the other on Sebastian. Afterwards, either in pairs or with the whole class, the pupils can compare notes and see how the two characters differ.

- Compare Act II Sc II and Act III Sc II and discover how the relationships between Caliban, Stephano and Trinculo change. From these changes, the pupils should be able to deduce characteristics of each of the three drunkards.

- Act V is tricky: it has wide stretches in which only a few characters speak, yet many people are on stage. Thinking about what these inactive characters are doing while the main speeches are taking place is a good exercise in the study of characteristics. Unlike a script, the Classical Comics graphic novel takes care of that, and you may want to consult the artwork in the book for ideas.

CHARACTER SHEETS:

There are many questions or issues that are central to each character. These can be given to the pupils in the form of a worksheet. Pupils should start on different questions and then work clockwise around the worksheet. After a set time, the whole class can compare their work and fill in any missing information or sections.

This resource provides character sheets for Prospero, Ariel, Caliban and Miranda (see pages 41 - 44).

EXPLORING CHARACTER - ACTIVITIES

STREAM OF CONSCIOUSNESS:

This form of writing attempts to copy thoughts exactly as they happen. It is therefore almost like looking into someone's brain. While there will be no action described as such (except when thinking about how to carry out a certain action, for example), stream of consciousness writing is a great tool for exploring a character's thoughts and therefore his or her personality. Here are some ideas:

- Imagine you are Caliban, Miranda, Ariel or Ferdinand immediately after Act I Sc II. What would you think about what has happened?
- From the point of view of one of the courtiers, write a reaction to the banquet scene and appearance of Ariel as harpy in Act III Sc III.
- Write Prospero's reaction to being ousted as Duke of Milan by Antonio.
- Pupils could imagine they are either Antonio or Sebastian and write their reactions and future plans after Act V Sc I.

BLANK COMIC SHEETS:

Pivotal moments of the play can also be used to explore emotions (and thus character) using blank comic pages. Instead of filling in what the characters are saying (Shakespeare tells us this, anyway), pupils can be asked to fill in what the characters are thinking, using thought bubbles and conforming to comic book layout rules (e.g. order of reading from top left to bottom right, bold writing to emphasise words in the text).

VENN DIAGRAMS:

Venn diagrams are used in logic and mathematics to show what various sets have in common. This technique can also be used to explore the similarities and differences (which can be as simple or complex as the pupils decide) of any three characters.

Split the class into groups and give each group a different set of three characters to analyse. Venn diagrams appear on page 45. Each group should be given some time to fill in its diagram. Then, each group looks at a Venn diagram that was completed by a different group. Give them some time to look at the diagram and to make comments on it. The comments can then be discussed and resolved in class.

OTHER ACTIVITIES:

Further ideas are:

- Prospero has often been compared to Shakespeare. In particular, Prospero's speech in Act V Sc I, when he bids his art farewell, has been seen as Shakespeare's swansong. Using a number of questions, the pupils could explore the parallels between the magician and the Bard. In this connection, the final chapter of Neil Gaiman's *Sandman* series (called *The Tempest* and collected in *The Wake*) might make interesting reading and a somewhat different point of reference.
  A further question might then be this: if Prospero is some form of vessel for Shakespeare, what conclusions might we be able to draw about Shakespeare's own character?
- Devise a speech for a character. Pupils should try not only to capture that person's character in the speech, but also his or her way of talking. This could include making sure the speech is in iambic pentameter (see page 50).
- For each of the characters, the pupils are to write a short, factual statement that sums up what they went on to do after the play ended (much like the notes before the end credits in the film *A Fish Called Wanda*). These can be either witty or serious, but they must fit the character. The best of these can be collected as "class end credits", or pupils can illustrate one of their end credits and thus provide panels (or storyboards) on the continuation of *The Tempest*.

PROSPERO'S RELATIONSHIPS

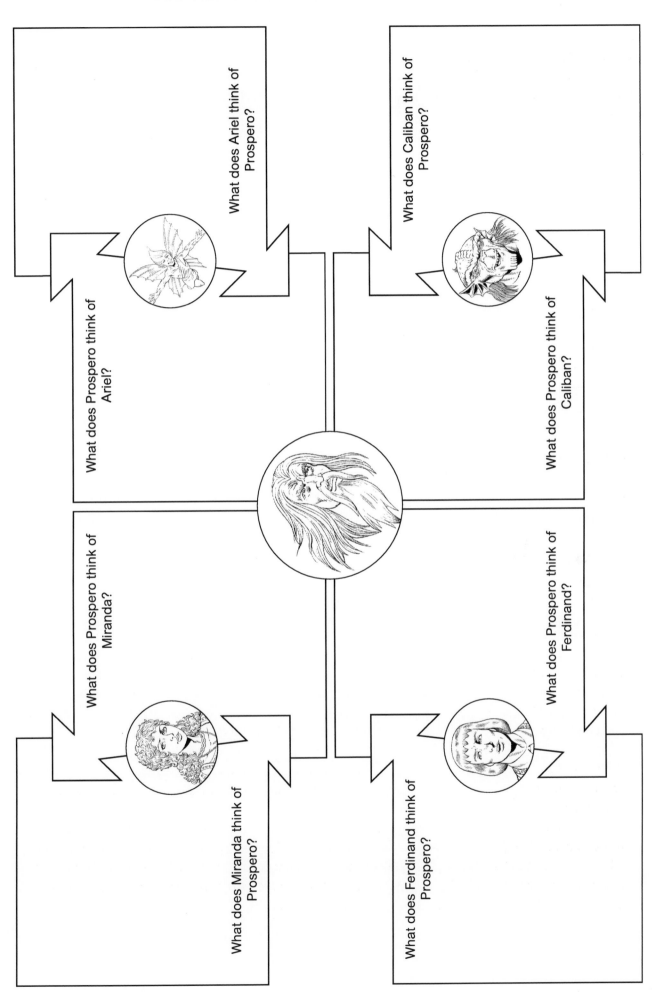

What does Ariel think of Prospero?

What does Caliban think of Prospero?

What does Prospero think of Ariel?

What does Prospero think of Caliban?

What does Prospero think of Miranda?

What does Prospero think of Ferdinand?

What does Miranda think of Prospero?

What does Ferdinand think of Prospero?

PROSPERO'S RELATIONSHIP WITH MIRANDA

(from **Act I Scene II**)

MIRANDA If by your art, my dearest father, you have Put the wild waters in this roar, allay them. The sky, it seems, would pour down stinking pitch, But that the sea, mounting to the welkin's cheek, Dashes the fire out. O, I have suffer'd With those that I saw suffer! a brave vessel, Who had, no doubt, some noble creature in her, Dash'd all to pieces. O, the cry did knock Against my very heart! poor souls, they perish'd. Had I been any god of power, I would Have sunk the sea within the earth, or ere It should the good ship so have swallow'd and The fraughting souls within her.	What does Miranda's first speech tell us about her feelings towards her father?
PROSPERO No harm. I have done nothing but in care of thee, Of thee, my dear one! thee, my daughter! who Art ignorant of what thou art, nought knowing Of whence I am, nor that I am more better Than Prospero, master of a full poor cell, And thy no greater father.	How might Prospero say this? What does that tell us about his relationship to Miranda?
PROSPERO 'Tis time I should inform thee further. [.] Sit down; ~~For thou must now know further.~~	Why has he not told her before?
MIRANDA You have often Begun to tell me what I am; but stopp'd And left me to a bootless inquisition, Concluding "Stay: not yet"	Prospero answers the question for her. What does this suggest?
MIRANDA Sir, are not you my father? **PROSPERO** Thy mother was a piece of virtue, and She said thou wast my daughter; and thy father Was Duke of Milan, and his only heir A princess;– no worse issued.	What does Prospero's ambiguous answer suggest about his relationship with Miranda?

PROSPERO'S RELATIONSHIP WITH MIRANDA

(cont'd)

PROSPERO My brother, and thy uncle, call'd Antonio – I pray thee, mark me, – that a brother should Be so perfidious! [...] Dost thou attend me? **MIRANDA** Sir, most heedfully. **PROSPERO** [...] Thou attend'st not. **MIRANDA** O, good sir! I do. **PROSPERO** I pray thee, mark me.	Why these constant admonitions to listen? What do they suggest about Miranda? and about Prospero?
MIRANDA Your tale, sir, would cure deafness.	How might Miranda say this? What does that tell us about her relationship with Prospero?
PROSPERO Well demanded, wench:	What does this response suggest about how Prospero views Miranda?
PROSPERO O, a cherubin Thou wast, that did preserve me. Thou didst smile, Infused with a fortitude from heaven, When I have deck'd the sea with drops full salt, Under my burden groan'd; which rais'd in me An undergoing stomach, to bear up Against what should ensue.	What does this tell us?
PROSPERO [...] Here cease more questions: Thou art inclin'd to sleep; 'tis a good dullness, And give it way: I know thou canst not choose. [*MIRANDA sleeps*]	Why does Prospero send his own daughter to sleep? What does that suggest?

PROSPERO'S RELATIONSHIP WITH ARIEL

(from **Act I Scene II**)

ARIEL All hail, great master! grave sir, hail! I come To answer thy best pleasure; be 't to fly, To swim, to dive into the fire, to ride On the curl'd clouds. To thy strong bidding, task Ariel, and all his quality.	How might Ariel say this? What does that tell us about his relationship with Prospero?
PROSPERO My brave spirit! Who was so firm, so constant, that this coil Would not infect his reason?	How might Prospero say this? What does that tell us about his relationship with Ariel?
PROSPERO Ariel, thy charge Exactly is perform'd: but there's more work. What is the time o' the day?	How does Prospero treat Ariel?
ARIEL Is there more toil? Since thou dost give me pains, Let me remember thee what thou hast promis'd, Which is not yet perform'd me.	What does this tell us about Ariel and how he sees Prospero?
ARIEL I pr'ythee, Remember, I have done thee worthy service; Told thee no lies, made thee no mistakings, serv'd Without or grudge or grumblings. Thou didst promise To bate me a full year.	What does this interchange tell us?
PROSPERO Dull thing, I say so; he, that Caliban, Whom now I keep in service.	Why does Prospero say this about Caliban? Although it reveals his attitude towards the monster, what does it also reveal about Prospero's relationship with Ariel?
ARIEL That's my noble master! What shall I do? say what? what shall I do? 	How does the interchange end? What does that tell us about Prospero and Ariel? Do you think Ariel is resentful? If so, what leads you to that conclusion?

PROSPERO'S RELATIONSHIP WITH CALIBAN

(from **Act I Scene II**)

PROSPERO But, as 'tis, We cannot miss him: he does make our fire, Fetch in our wood and serves in offices That profit us. What, ho! Slave! Caliban! Thou earth, thou! Speak. [...]	What do we immediately learn about the relationship between Caliban and Prospero?
CALIBAN As wicked dew as e'er my mother brush'd With raven's feather from unwholesome fen, Drop on you both! a south-west blow on ye, And blister you all o'er!	How does Caliban treat Prospero?
PROSPERO For this, be sure, to-night thou shalt have cramps, Side-stitches that shall pen thy breath up; urchins Shall forth at vast of night, that they may work All exercise on thee; thou shalt be pinch'd As thick as honey-comb, each pinch more stinging Than bees that made them.	Why does Prospero act like this?
CALIBAN I must eat my dinner. This island's mine, by Sycorax my mother, Which thou tak'st from me. When thou camest first Thou strok'dst me, and mad'st much of me; wouldst give me Water with berries in't; and teach me how To name the bigger light, and how the less, That burn by day and night: and then I lov'd thee And show'd thee all the qualities o' th' isle, The fresh springs, brine-pits, barren place and fertile; Cursed be I that did so! All the charms Of Sycorax, toads, beetles, bats, light on you! For I am all the subjects that you have, Which first was mine own king: and here you sty me In this hard rock, whiles you do keep from me The rest o' th' island.	What does Caliban accuse Prospero of? What does he hope to gain thereby?
PROSPERO Thou most lying slave, Whom stripes may move, not kindness! I have us'd thee, Filth as thou art, with human care; and lodg'd thee In mine own cell, till thou didst seek to violate The honour of my child.	Who do you think is right? Why?

PROSPERO'S RELATIONSHIP WITH CALIBAN

(cont'd)

MIRANDA Abhorred slave, Which any print of goodness wilt not take, Being capable of all ill! I pitied thee, Took pains to make thee speak, taught thee each hour One thing or other: when thou didst not, savage, Know thine own meaning, but wouldst gabble like A thing most brutish, I endow'd thy purposes With words that made them known. But thy vile race, Though thou didst learn, had that in't which good natures Could not abide to be with; therefore wast thou Deservedly confin'd into this rock, Who hadst deserv'd more than a prison.	These lines are often assigned to Prospero. Whose character do you think they fit best? Explain your answer.
PROSPERO Hag-seed, hence! Fetch us in fuel; and be quick, thou'rt best, To answer other business. Shrug'st thou, malice? If thou neglect'st, or dost unwillingly What I command, I'll rack thee with old cramps, Fill all thy bones with aches, make thee roar, That beasts shall tremble at thy din.	Is Prospero right to treat Caliban like this?

PROSPERO'S RELATIONSHIP WITH FERDINAND

(from **Act I Scene II**)

PROSPERO How? the best? What wert thou, if the King of Naples heard thee?	Why does Prospero mention the King of Naples, when Ferdinand never did?
PROSPERO [Aside] The Duke of Milan, And his more braver daughter could control thee, If now 'twere fit to do 't. At the first sight They have chang'd eyes. Delicate Ariel, I'll set thee free for this! [To FERDINAND] A word, good sir; I fear you have done yourself some wrong: a word.	Prospero makes a number of asides when talking to Ferdinand. What does this suggest?
PROSPERO Soft, sir! one word more. [Aside] They are both in either's powers: but this swift business I must uneasy make, lest too light winning Make the prize light. [To FERDINAND] One word more; I charge thee, That thou attend me: thou dost here usurp The name thou ow'st not; and hast put thyself Upon this island as a spy, to win it From me, the lord on 't.	Prospero constantly repeats "one word". What does this suggest about the relationship between Prospero and Ferdinand?
PROSPERO [To FERDINAND] Follow me. [To MIRANDA]Speak not you for him; he's a traitor. [To FERDINAND] Come; I'll manacle thy neck and feet together: Sea-water shalt thou drink; thy food shall be The fresh-brook mussels, wither'd roots and husks Wherein the acorn cradled. Follow.	How does Prospero portray himself here? To what extent is this true to his real character?
FERDINAND So they are: My spirits, as in a dream, are all bound up. My father's loss, the weakness which I feel, The wrack of all my friends, nor this man's threats, To whom I am subdued, are but light to me, Might I but through my prison once a day Behold this maid: all corners else o' th' earth Let liberty make use of; space enough Have I in such a prison.	What does Ferdinand's reaction reveal about his character and what he thinks of Prospero?

ANTONIO AND SEBASTIAN PLOT TO KILL ALONSO
(from **Act II Scene I**)

ANTONIO

They fell together all, as by consent;
They dropp'd, as by a thunder-stroke. What might,
Worthy Sebastian – O! what might – No more:–
And yet, methinks, I see it in thy face,
What thou shouldst be: the occasion speaks thee, and
My strong imagination sees a crown
Dropping upon thy head.

SEBASTIAN

What! art thou waking?

ANTONIO

Do you not hear me speak?

SEBASTIAN

I do; and surely
It is a sleepy language, and thou speak'st
Out of thy sleep. What is it thou didst say?

[...]

ANTONIO

Noble Sebastian,
Thou let'st thy fortune sleep – die, rather; wink'st
Whiles thou art waking. [...] O!
If you but knew how you the purpose cherish
Whiles thus you mock it! how, in stripping it,
You more invest it! Ebbing men, indeed,
Most often do so near the bottom run
By their own fear or sloth.

SEBASTIAN

Pr'ythee, say on;
The setting of thine eye and cheek proclaim
A matter from thee, and a birth, indeed,
Which throes thee much to yield.

ANTONIO

Thus, sir.
Although this lord [...] hath here almost persuaded,--
For he's a spirit of persuasion, only
Professes to persuade,--the King his son's alive,
'Tis as impossible that he's undrown'd
And he that sleeps here, swims.

SEBASTIAN

I have no hope
That he's undrown'd.

> Did the plot just suggest itself to Antonio, or was he only waiting for the right moment?

> What do Sebastian's references to sleep suggest?

> Why does Antonio call Sebastian an "ebbing" man?

> Does Sebastian really not understand? What does this suggest?

> Is "hope" the right word to be spoken by Sebastian?

ANTONIO

O! out of that 'no hope'
What great hope have you! no hope, that way, is
Another way so high a hope, that even
Ambition cannot pierce a wink beyond,
But doubt discovery there. Will you grant with me,
That Ferdinand is drown'd?

> In what way might Antonio say this?

SEBASTIAN

He's gone.

ANTONIO

Then, tell me,
Who's the next heir of Naples?

> What does the way Sebastian and Antonio finish each other's lines suggest?

SEBASTIAN

Claribel.

ANTONIO

She that is Queen of Tunis; she that dwells
Ten leagues beyond man's life; she that from Naples
Can have no note, [...] till new-born chins
Be rough and razorable; she that from whom
We all were sea-swallow'd, though some cast again,
And by that destiny to perform an act
Whereof what's past is prologue, what to come,
In yours and my discharge.

> Why does Antonio speak so obliquely?

SEBASTIAN

What stuff is this! How say you?
'Tis true, my brother's daughter's Queen of Tunis;
So is she heir of Naples; 'twixt which regions
There is some space.

> What might Sebastian be thinking?

ANTONIO

A space whose every cubit
Seems to cry out, 'How shall that Claribel
Measure us back to Naples? Keep in Tunis,
And let Sebastian wake!' Say, this were death
That now hath seiz'd them; why, they were no worse
Than now they are. There be that can rule Naples
As well as he that sleeps; [...] O, that you bore
The mind that I do! What a sleep were this
For your advancement! Do you understand me?

> How does Antonio try to persuade Sebastian?

SEBASTIAN

Methinks I do.

ANTONIO

And how does your content
Tender your own good fortune?

SEBASTIAN

I remember,
You did supplant your brother Prospero.

ANTONIO

True:
And look how well my garments sit upon me;
Much feater than before. My brother's servants
Were then my fellows; now they are my men.

SEBASTIAN

But, for your conscience.

> What does Sebastian's interjection suggest?

ANTONIO

Ay, sir; where lies that? if 'twere a kibe,
'Twould put me to my slipper; but I feel not
This deity in my bosom: twenty consciences,
That stand 'twixt me and Milan, candied be they
And melt, ere they molest! Here lies your brother,
No better than the earth he lies upon,
If he were that which now he's like – that's dead –
Whom I, with this obedient steel, three inches of it,
Can lay to bed for ever – whiles you, doing thus,
To the perpetual wink for aye might put
This ancient morsel, this Sir Prudence, who
Should not upbraid our course. For all the rest,
They'll take suggestion as a cat laps milk;
They'll tell the clock to any business that
We say befits the hour.

> What does Antonio suggest about his conscience? To what degree is this true for everyone?

SEBASTIAN

Thy case, dear friend,
Shall be my precedent; as thou got'st Milan,
I'll come by Naples. Draw thy sword: one stroke
Shall free thee from the tribute which thou pay'st;
And I the king shall love thee.

> What are the arguments that persuade Sebastian? To what extent would they persuade you, if you were Sebastian?

ANTONIO

Draw together;
And when I rear my hand, do you the like,
To fall it on Gonzalo.

> What does this line from Sebastian suggest?

SEBASTIAN

O! but one word.

[They talk apart] [...]

ANTONIO

Then let us both be sudden.

> To what might Antonio be replying?

PROSPERO CHARACTER SHEET

Prospero's name means "I cause to succeed, I make fortunate." Does this match his personality?

Is Prospero a cruel master?

Is Prospero a good father?

What kind of a person would Prospero be without his magic?

ARIEL CHARACTER SHEET

Ariel is an airy spirit. What does this suggest about Ariel?

Does Ariel like serving Prospero?

Is Ariel more or less human than Prospero?

What gender do you think Ariel is? In what way might gender influence our view of Ariel?

CALIBAN CHARACTER SHEET

Caliban is very earthbound. What does this suggest about Caliban?

Is Caliban a victim or an aggressor?

To what extent is Caliban the opposite of other characters?

What would Caliban do if the island were his?

MIRANDA CHARACTER SHEET

Miranda means "to be wondered at." In what way might she be wonderful or admirable?

Is Miranda truly a pure and innocent damsel?

Does Miranda give in too easily to Ferdinand?

Do you think Miranda would make a good wife?

VENN DIAGRAMS

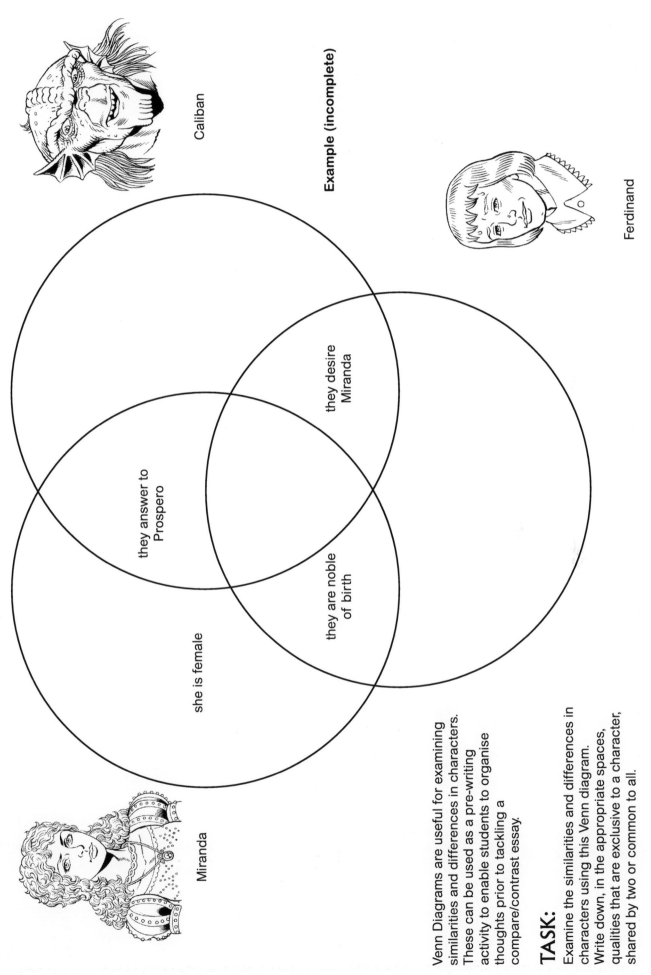

Caliban

Example (incomplete)

Ferdinand

they desire
Miranda

they answer to
Prospero

they are noble
of birth

she is female

Miranda

Venn Diagrams are useful for examining
similarities and differences in characters.
These can be used as a pre-writing
activity to enable students to organise
thoughts prior to tackling a
compare/contrast essay.

TASK:

Examine the similarities and differences in
characters using this Venn diagram.
Write down, in the appropriate spaces,
qualities that are exclusive to a character,
shared by two or common to all.

VENN DIAGRAMS

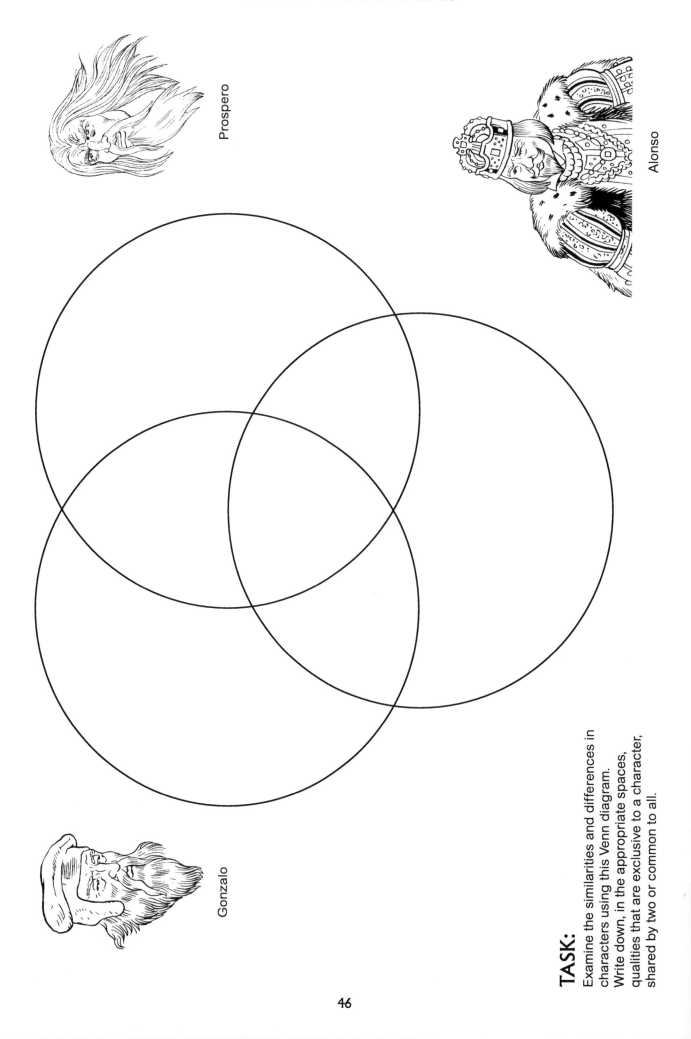

Prospero

Alonso

Gonzalo

TASK:

Examine the similarities and differences in characters using this Venn diagram.
Write down, in the appropriate spaces, qualities that are exclusive to a character, shared by two or common to all.

VENN DIAGRAMS

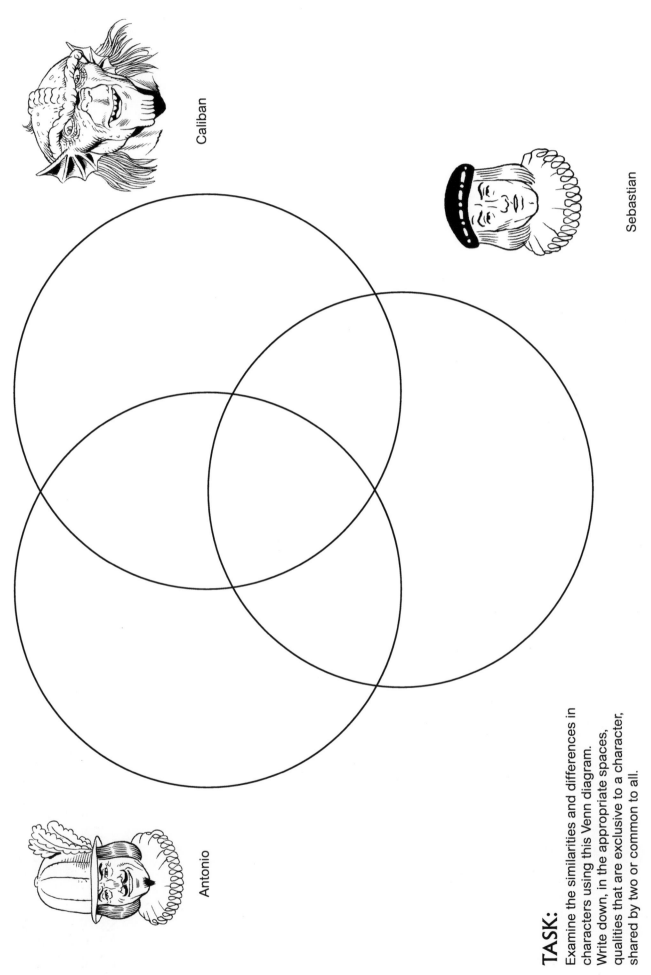

Caliban

Sebastian

Antonio

TASK:

Examine the similarities and differences in characters using this Venn diagram.
Write down, in the appropriate spaces, qualities that are exclusive to a character, shared by two or common to all.

47

VENN DIAGRAMS

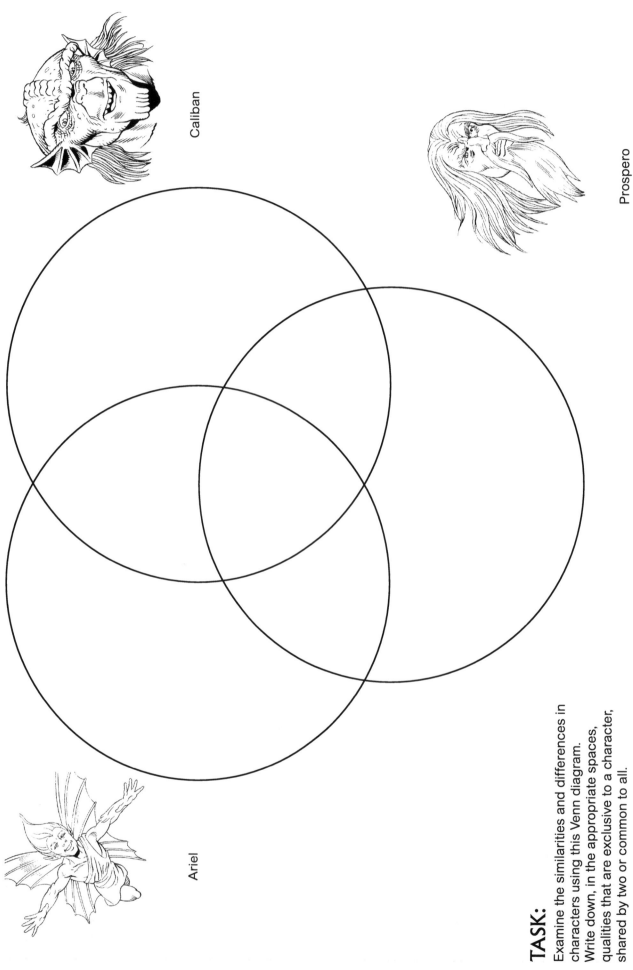

Caliban

Prospero

Ariel

TASK:

Examine the similarities and differences in characters using this Venn diagram.
Write down, in the appropriate spaces, qualities that are exclusive to a character, shared by two or common to all.

SHAKESPEARE'S LANGUAGE

Introduction

Apart from Shakespeare's wide and diverse vocabulary and somewhat unusual diction or word order, the two main issues that pupils find difficult with Shakespeare are the prosody (verse structure) of his writing and the imagery.

The vocabulary issue can only be tackled with a glossary or dictionary, although some knowledge of foreign languages (especially French and Latin) may help. The difficulty students have with the word order is more baffling, especially as most pupils have no difficulty comprehending what Yoda (of *Star Wars* fame) says. Patience must be the answer here.

Prosody:

When writing in verse, Shakespeare usually employs iambic pentameter. This means that each line contains five metric feet: in this case five iambs. An iamb consists of two syllables, the first one being unstressed, and the second stressed (ti-TUM). The basic line of Shakespearean poetry, then, has ten syllables and scans as follows (each "X" representing a syllable):

x	>X<	x	>X<	x	>X<	x	>X<	x	>X<

e.g. (from Act I Scene II, line 14)

No	more	a-	maze-	ment.	Tell	your	pit-	eous	heart

Although the lines in Shakespeare's plays appear in verse form, they usually don't rhyme, and as such they are "blank verse".

Interestingly, Shakespeare's lines aren't always pure iambic pentameter. Sometimes there is an extra syllable. Depending on where this extra syllable is and whether it is stressed or unstressed, it can either be an unstressed monosyllabic foot added on to the end of the line (basically just one extra syllable added on that doesn't fit the meter) or an anapaest mixed in among the iambs. An anapaest consists of three syllables, of which only the last is stressed (ti-ti-TUM). As the stress is on the last syllable, anapaests mix well with iambs.

The following line (Act I Scene II, line 6) has a monosyllabic foot added onto the end:

x	>X<	x	>X<	x	>X<	x	>X<	x	>X<	x
With	those	that	I	saw	suff-	er!	A	brave	vess-	el

This line (Act III Scene III Line 55) has an anapaest as the fifth foot:

x	>X<	x	>X<	x	>X<	x	>X<	x	x	>X<
And	what	is	in't,	the	ne-	ver-	sur	feit-	ed	sea

Sometimes it is not easy to decide whether the last foot is an anapaest or an iamb with a monosyllabic foot tagged on (e.g. Act I Scene II, lines 1 or 7); this depends on where the stress lies.

Metric stress does not always match emphasis when speaking. In this line (Act I Scene II, line 2) they differ quite starkly at the beginning, showing that, although the number of syllables are correct for an iambic pentameter, it wouldn't be spoken in that way and therefore it breaks the iambic framework.

x	>X<	x	>X<	x	>X<	x	>X<	x	>X<	x
Put	the	wild	wat-	ers	in	this	roar,	all-	ay	them

THE RHYTHM OF SHAKESPEARE'S LANGUAGE
"wouldst gabble like a thing most brutish"

Use the grid below to help you transform the following lines of Ariel's speech as harpy from Act III Scene III into iambic pentameter. The rhythm for this is written down at the top of the table. Each syllable should occupy one box. Remember that not every line has to be pure iambic pentameter.

ARIEL: *You are three men of sin, whom Destiny,*
(That hath to instrument this lower world
And what is in't), the never-surfeited sea
Hath caus'd to belch up you; and on this island,
Where man doth not inhabit, you 'mongst men
Being most unfit to live. I have made you mad;
And even with such-like valour men hang and drown
Their proper selves.

x	>X<	x	>X<	x	>X<	x	>X<	x	>X<	

SHAKESPEARE'S LANGUAGE

Imagery:

Some of the beauty of Shakespeare's language (as well as its difficulty) stems from his daring and original use of imagery. The main techniques used (and that present problems to pupils) are similes and metaphors. It is important to bear in mind that both utilise imagery and compare one thing to another; their effectiveness and strength is derived from the degree to which the first named element is similar to the second element. The more effective the image, the more levels it will work on and the more it will challenge received opinion or cliché.

Some ideas for work on language are:

- Look at what kind of language each character uses. Analyse how Prospero's language differs from Caliban's, for example. Alternatively, pupils could examine how various characters butt into each other's conversation or finish off lines for each other (e.g. Antonio and Sebastian).
- Ferdinand's main feature of speaking is antithesis – when he talks, he often uses opposites in close proximity to convey his message. Pupils could take his first speech in Act III Scene I and highlight the opposites, then practise delivering the speech, emphasising those opposites.
- After pupils have discovered the main features of a character's speech, they could try their own hand at writing some dialogue for that character, staying within the framework for that personality. Advanced pupils could write this dialogue in iambic pentameter, or even within a rhyming pattern.
- To discover the rhythm of Shakespeare's lines, students can practise splitting the lines up into the syllables and then discovering where the stresses are, using pure iambic pentameter as a guideline. Once they have understood the concept, they can write a few lines of their own iambic pentameter.
- For more focused work on imagery, pupils can be asked to search for a number of similes and metaphors and explain their effect. They should start by analysing what the second element means and then consider how this relates to the first element. From this work, pupils should be able to assess the degree to which the imagery is effective (because of the similarities).
- Shakespeare is also famous for his unusual and inventive insults. While *The Tempest* doesn't contain the best, it does boast a good number. For a more fun activity, pupils can search these out (Act I, Scenes I and II are good places to start) and then hurl them at each other.
- To discover the ways in which a detailed analysis of language can be used (and abused) to support arguments, pupils could invent a theory about Shakespeare (e.g. he secretly hated the king and the whole idea of a monarchy) and see if they can find support for their theory in the text (e.g. Gonzalo's Commonwealth speech).

The essay framework contained in the chapter on Themes (page 56) can be used to help collect information, if a formal essay is to be the outcome.

Classical Comics Teaching Resource: *The Tempest*

FERDINAND'S LABOURS
"My language? Heavens!"

Use this sheet to explore the opposites in Ferdinand's speech in Act III Scene I. Each underlined word has an opposite. Find the opposite from the words at the bottom and write it in the correct place (without referring to a copy of the play)!

There be some <u>sports</u> are <u>painful</u>, and their _____

_____ in them sets off: some kinds of <u>baseness</u>

Are _____ undergone, and most <u>poor</u> matters

Point to _____ ends. This my mean task

Would be as heavy to me as odious, but

The mistress which I serve <u>quickens</u> what's _____

And makes my <u>labours</u> _____; O, she is

Ten times more <u>gentle</u> than her father's crabbed,

And he's compos'd of _____. I must remove

Some thousands of these logs, and pile them up,

Upon a <u>sore</u> injunction: my _____ mistress

Weeps when she sees me work; and says, such baseness

Had never like executor.

Word	Its opposite
sports	
painful	
baseness	
poor	
quickens	
labours	
gentle	
sore	

nobly   **harshness**   **delight**   **pleasures**

rich   **labour**   **dead**   **sweet**

POETIC COMPARISON IN *THE TEMPEST*
"The baseless fabric of this vision"

Shakespeare often used similes (comparisons using "like" or "as [adjective] as a [noun]") and metaphors (comparisons stating that something *is* something else, rather than that it is "like" it) to convey his message and to make his language more effective and interesting. Both techniques rely on commonalities between the two things being compared.

For example: *The grass was like an emerald (simile)*

The effectiveness of the simile depends on the grass being similar to an emerald. This can be displayed using a diagram:

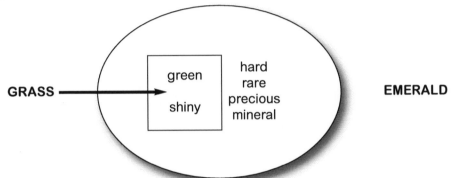

As this illustration reveals, grass is mostly unlike an emerald. The only characteristics they share are "green" and "shiny". Most of the other elements that make up an emerald actually contradict what grass is. The simile is therefore not a very good one (it has also been overused).

Good comparisons, be they similes or metaphors, will usually reveal a number of things in common and also provide some new and startling insight into the object being described. Look at this simile from *The Tempest:*

He receives comfort like cold porridge (Act II Scene I, line 10)

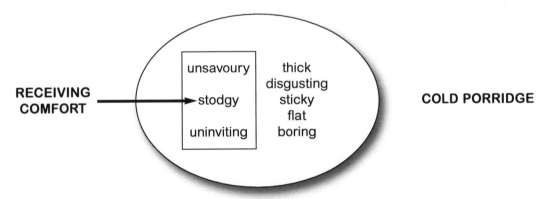

The comparison here is to being comforted and to receiving (having to eat) cold porridge. We can imagine, due to the characteristics of cold porridge listed above, how Alonso reacts to the comfort, even down to his facial expression. Comfort is obviously a meal he doesn't enjoy. Apart from a range of similarities, the comparison is also unusual – the hallmark of effective imagery.

Metaphors follow the same principle, but the comparison is more direct. *The Tempest* is sparse when it comes to direct metaphors. It is said that the whole play is a metaphor and therefore such literary devices are not needed. However, the most famous metaphor from the play is Prospero's speech, "We are such stuff/ As dreams are made on ; and our little life / Is rounded with a sleep."

POETIC COMPARISON IN *THE TEMPEST*

Now that you know how poetic comparisons work, try for yourself by analysing the use of comparisons in *The Tempest*.

Comparison:_____(simile/metaphor)

first element   **second element**

_____   _____

_____

Explain the effectiveness:

_____

_____

_____

_____

Comparison:_____(simile/metaphor)

first element   **second element**

_____   _____

_____

Explain the effectiveness:

_____

_____

_____

_____

INSULTING PROSPERO AND CALIBAN

"You taught me language; and my profit on't is, I know how to curse."

Use the following grid to jot down the insults Prospero and Caliban exchange (starting at Act I Scene II).
Can you find any other insults in the play?

Once you have collected a number of insults, you can try them out in pairs. But rather than just shout the insults at each other, try to be in character – how would Prospero say the insults? How would Caliban say them?

Prospero vs Caliban	Caliban vs Prospero

Use this grid to jot down any other insults you come across in *The Tempest*.

Who says the insult?	To whom?	What is the insult?

EXPLORING THEMES

Introduction

This chapter focuses on the main themes of *The Tempest*. They are (in order of presentation):

- Betrayal and Forgiveness
- Colonisation
- Fate and Justice
- Legitimate Rule and Social Order
- Magic
- Slavery and Servitude

Some themes overlap: work on Colonisation will also be of use when examining Slavery and Servitude; the theme of Betrayal and Forgiveness is akin to the topic of Fate and Justice. These similarities are invitations to explore the themes and their interconnections further. Some themes also interlink with character work; once again, this is an invitation to work broadly and approach one topic from a number of different angles.

Setting the Themes

The beginning of a play – much like the beginning of any story, novel or film – has to fulfil a number of functions. First and foremost, it must grab the attention of the viewer/reader while, usually, the main characters are presented along with the main themes.

Curiously, *The Tempest* opens with a storm at sea and presents mainly secondary characters. Although this is unusual, many of the themes that are important in the play are at least hinted at in the introductory scene. Also, if we take the opening also to encompass lines 1-32 of Act I Scene II, then we have a much richer backdrop of character and themes.

EXPLORING THEMES

(Act I Scene I and Act I Scene II, lines 1-32)

TASK:

Working in pairs or small groups, use the following table to explore to what extent the themes of *The Tempest*, listed to the left of the page, are already present in the opening scene(s) of the play. Remember to provide evidence from the play for your thoughts and to explain in what way the quotation you have selected foreshadows the theme.

Two rows have been left blank so that you can add any additional themes that you identify.

Themes	Evidence from the text	Explain relevance of evidence
justice & fate		
magic		
colonisation		
legitimate rule & social order		

BETRAYAL AND FORGIVENESS

"The rarer action is in virtue than in vengeance"

Prospero means the events that take place in the play to be a journey of realisation, repentance and punishment resulting in forgiveness for past betrayals. This is his plan for the courtiers, although the audience does not know right until the very end whether Prospero ultimately plans to forgive the three men of sin or punish them. Indeed, it seems that forgiveness was not his original plan – the idea being given to him by Ariel.

The solution the play presents to deal with betrayal is a process of realisation and "moral cleansing" before forgiveness can realistically happen. Even Prospero learns that forgiveness must be unconditional – which is why he is unaffected by the lack of remorse shown by his betrayers.

TASK:

In the following table, identify who is betrayed by whom (or who <u>was</u> betrayed by whom) and fill in the details. Try to give references to support your answer.

Characters	How?	What was their motive for betrayal?	Are they forgiven?	Do they regret their actions?
Prospero betrays Ariel	By delaying his freedom (Act I, Sc II, 242-249)	Because he needed Ariel to carry out his demands	Yes	No
Alonso betrayed _____				
Sebastian tries to betray _____				
Antonio betrayed _____				
Antonio tries to betray _____				
Gonzalo betrayed _____				
Caliban betrays _____				

COLONISATION

"One of them is a plain fish and no doubt marketable"

One of the sources of Shakespeare's *Tempest* is the report by William Strachey of the voyage of Sir George Somers to the Jamestown colony in Virginia. In the course of this trip, one ship, the *Sea Venture*, was shipwrecked on Bermuda. The survivors subsequently established a colony and lived there for a year. Some sailors mutinied because they wanted to stay on the island, preferring its insular paradise to the North American colony.

The endeavour to colonise the New World forms a backdrop for the action, but even a cursory glance makes it clear that colonisation soon becomes a central theme, tied in with the issue of legitimate and proper governance.

Caliban is the "native" and is thus subject to the various practices of colonisation. Stephano and Trinculo befuddle him with alcohol, all the while wondering how they can get him back to Italy alive to make their fortune from displaying him. Interestingly enough, this is the same reaction Sebastian and Antonio have to Caliban. Prospero becomes his master and uses him as a slave, also taking his territory. The treatment of Caliban reflects the attitude towards and treatment of New World natives by the West.

However, it is unclear to what extent Shakespeare criticises this. While Caliban nowadays is mostly portrayed as the "noble savage" who has had his homeland taken away and is therefore justifiably vengeful, it seems that earlier audiences saw him as a creature, or brute (described as "savage and deformed slave") who benefitted from the introduction of Western civilisation and culture. His refusal to accept such civilisation was seen as the reaction of an animal, not that of a human being who resents his land being overrun.

Ultimately, this question remains subject to individual interpretation; however, Gonzalo's musings on the perfect state (in Act II Sc I, including reference to "plantation"), suggest that Shakespeare may have thought that not everything was going as it should in the new colonies (although Gonzalo's speech can also be interpreted ironically).

Discussion points:

- To whom does the island in *The Tempest* belong?
- Based on the evidence in the text (which is not wholly satisfactory), determine the order of colonisation of the island.
- Consider the colonisation of America. When America was "discovered" by Christopher Columbus in 1492 (just over 100 years before *The Tempest* was written), was the land uninhabited?
- How did that compare with the arrival of Romans in Britain 2,000 years ago?
- Why do we consider that to be an invasion, as opposed to a discovery?

COLONISATION AND ACQUIRING LAND

The question of who owns the island underpins the relationship between Prospero and Caliban. Caliban feels that Prospero stole the island from him. Use the grid below to discover to what extent historical questions of acquisition and ownership of land are reflected in *The Tempest*.

Question	Answer	Relevance to *The Tempest*
Was Bermuda inhabited before the English arrived, or did another country have a claim to priority?		
What methods are there generally for claiming "new" land?		
What is the basis for claiming land in a colony?		
In what way – if at all – were the natives given any form of compensation?		

THE COLONISATION OF THE ISLAND

There are a number of "waves" of colonisation of the island. Caliban states, "This island's mine by Sycorax my mother" (Act I Scene II, line 333); Prospero does not agree with that. Is Caliban right? To whom does the island belong, and why? Use this sheet to explore the order of colonisation and thus to discover who might have the best claim to ownership of the island. Use Act I Scene II, lines 251-295 as your main source.
Use lines to link the faces to the order in which they arrived.

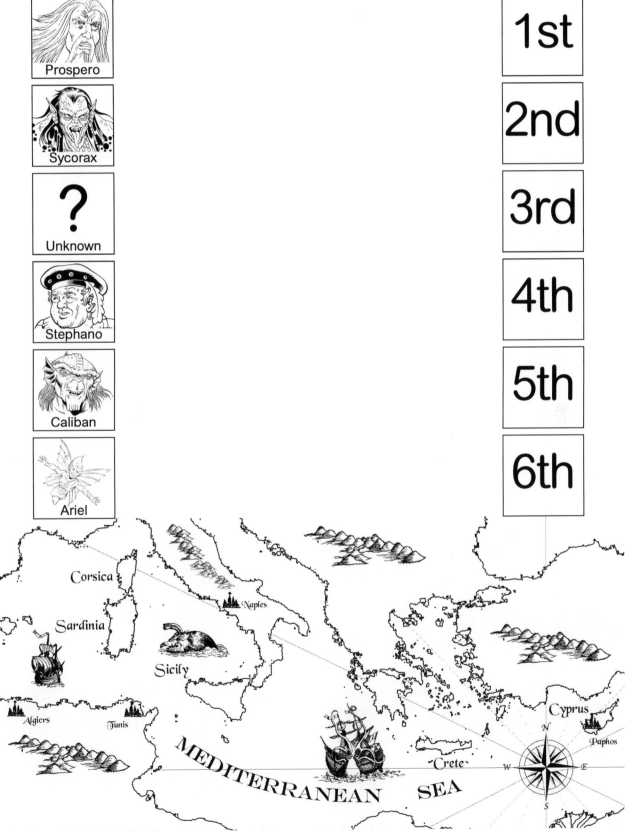

THE COLONISATION OF THE ISLAND

Even if we know the order of arrival on the island, it doesn't necessarily address the issue of its ownership. What action(s) need(s) to be taken to obtain ownership? Have any of the characters carried out these actions? Use the grid below to help you decide who owns the island.

Action	Character	Relevance of Action for Ownership
Cultivated the island		
Enslaved the inhabitants of the island		
Defended the island against aggressors		
Born on the island		
Built up a structure of legislation, jurisdiction and administration		
Explored (and charted) the island		

THE SHIPWRECK ON BERMUDA

The Tempest starts with the ship bearing the Italian courtiers foundering and breaking in a storm. The passengers make it to the island where Prospero lives. Many commentators have noted the similarity of this part of the plot and the shipwreck of the *Sea Venture* on Bermuda. Use the grid below to discover the degree to which Shakespeare retells the events of the *Sea Venture*.

Question	Answer
To what extent does the account of the storm match or differ from Shakespeare's description?	
What names contained in Strachey's report crop up again in *The Tempest*? Why do you think this might be?	
To what extent is the description of Bermuda similar or different to the island?	
What do all these clues and parallels suggest about the setting and the theme of the play?	

ALCOHOL AND COLONISATION

The contact of the civilised courtiers with the strange native, Caliban, is marked in *The Tempest* by the abundance of alcohol. Use the grid below to discover to what extent this mirrors the experience of the natives in North America when faced with the (English) settlers.

Question	Answer	Relevance to *The Tempest*
Did the natives know alcohol before the arrival of the settlers?		
What was alcohol primarily used for by the natives?		
Was alcohol used purposefully by the settlers?		
In what way was alcohol detrimental to the natives?		

FATE AND JUSTICE

"Destiny, that hath to instrument this lower world"

Fate and justice are recurrent themes of *The Tempest*. The two are linked: to what extent does fate punish sin, and to what degree are we accountable for our actions, either in this life or the next? Indeed, the main plot of the play is about Prospero exacting some form of revenge for being usurped as the Duke of Milan. As carefully as Prospero manages the various characters to achieve his aim with maximum effect, there are factors that are beyond his control and must be left to fate. There are two main instances in which destiny could be said to have enabled Prospero's plans to come to fruition and that he was unable to control with his magic. The first is the arrival of Miranda and him on the island "by providence divine" (Act I Scene II, line 160), the second is the royal wedding that forced his "victims" to pass in close proximity to the island "By accident most strange" (Act I Scene II, line 179), enabling Prospero to cast his tempest on their ship, thus setting off the chain of events that we see in the play. Central to Prospero's designs is the speech given by Ariel in the guise of a harpy* after the fairy banquet has vanished. Here Prospero, although orchestrating the punishment of the sinners throughout, presents the harpy as a minister of fate – precisely what Ariel is not. It therefore seems important to Prospero that Alonso, Antonio and Sebastian believe themselves to be punished by some higher power, rather than a mere human. It is impossible to know whether the "three men of sin" would actually have been punished (by fate) if Prospero had not intervened (indeed, in the play Prospero does not punish Antonio and Sebastian for their plot to do away with Alonso), nor does he punish Antonio or Alonso for their wrongdoings in ousting him from Milan in the first place.

Note, also, how Prospero is both judge and jury (cf. Lewis Carroll's poem *The Mouse's Tale* from chapter 3 of *Alice's Adventures in Wonderland*)

TASKS:

Analyse Ariel's speech in Act III Scene III looking for the themes of fate and justice.

If we take Ariel as representing fate, is he fair and just?
(Remember that Alonso believes that his son is dead at this point)

Is fate always just and fair?

How would Alonso have felt, being a king, yet dictated to by a stronger power than he?

At this point, Alonso seems to have been punished more than Antonio, yet it was Antonio who ousted his brother Prospero in the first place. Is this fair?
On top of this, Antonio is the least remorseful. Do you think that is because of his character, or because he is the least punished?

*This keys in with the myth of Phineas, a prophet, who revealed too much about the plans of the gods and was therefore punished by Zeus. Alone on an island, he had a banquet in front of him which he could never eat because the harpies would steal it from him.

EXPLORING ARIEL AS MINISTER OF FATE

Use the questions in the following table to help you examine Ariel's speech in Act III Scene III, lines 53-82, and assess the extent that Ariel – were he truly to be a minister of fate – is fair and just.

Punishment ordained by Ariel	Would this be fair? Why?	How would your ideal punishment be different (if at all)?
The tempest and the wrecking of the ship as punishment for setting Prospero and Miranda adrift		
The King and his courtiers were driven crazy as punishment for their wrongdoings against Prospero		
Slow ruin on the island as punishment for the twelve years of exile endured by Prospero		

LEGITIMATE RULE AND SOCIAL ORDER

"The government I cast upon my brother, and to my state grew stranger"

One of the main preoccupations of the play is legitimacy of rule and the perfect form of governance. We see this not only in the two usurping brothers (Antonio usurped his brother Prospero, and Sebastian showed his intention to usurp his brother Alonso), but also in Gonzalo's dream of the institution of the perfect state on the island with him as king – which he talks about in front of his own king! It is also touched upon in Stephano's anticipation of kingship on the island, with Trinculo and Caliban as his viceroys.

From the start of the play, we learn that social order is under question, as
the Boatswain (a common man) orders the king and courtiers to stay below deck.

Prospero's account of his loss of the dukedom, recounted to Miranda for the benefit of the audience, is the main story of an enforced change to authority. As such, it has a particular importance as blueprint for all the other intended or past usurpations. It also begs the question of whether Prospero was rightfully deposed – or, if not rightfully, at least for good reason. After all, Prospero himself admits to not having been a good duke (although he still maintains that the people loved him). Gonzalo's ideas for rule, intended to cheer up King Alonso after the supposed death of his son, is fraught with difficulties, as it mixes up Utopia, El Dorado and even a form of communism – the very fact that Gonzalo is ruler of a country without a ruler is so blatant a contradiction that Sebastian picks up on it immediately.

Stephano's idea of kingship is characteristically straightforward. He has no great plans – kingship, with its power and the accompanying apparel, seem enough for him. Indeed, it seems the apparel in itself is sufficient, as this alone stops him from carrying out his plan.

The desire to rule, or to be ruled by a "friendly" king, drives two sub-plots of *The Tempest*: Antonio persuades Sebastian to follow his example and to claim the kingship from his own brother, while Caliban persuades Stephano to kill his hated master.

Throughout the play, no ruler's position or status seems to be safe, and we are reminded that any post of authority is only temporary. As Prospero muses in Act IV, Sc I, l152-158, nothing in this life is permanent.

TASK:

Imagine you are a candidate to be the next ruler of your country. You will have complete control over everything, as long as you are voted into power.

Write a brief manifesto that outlines any changes you would make. Justify each change with a reason, and list the benefits that would occur. You may want to consider some things that would convince people to vote for you (so-called "vote-winners"). Once elected, you will also need to consider measures that will protect you from any challenger.

PROSPERO IS OUSTED FROM MILAN

TASK:

Read Act I, Sc II, lines 66-151

("My brother and thy uncle" ... "Did us but loving wrong.") and answer the following questions:

- To what extent is neglect a valid reason to depose a ruler?

- How does Antonio go about taking over the dukedom? Do you think this was planned long before Prospero was ousted?

- Why does Antonio take over the dukedom? Does he act maliciously?

- How important is it for a kingdom/dukedom to be independent? List the advantages and disadvantages.

- Do you think the people really loved Prospero as their ruler? Explain your answer.

GONZALO DREAMS OF THE PERFECT STATE

(Act II, Scene I, ll. 142-168)

GONZALO
    Had I plantation of this isle, my lord,--
 	
ANTONIO
    He'd sow 't with nettle-seed.
 	
SEBASTIAN
    Or docks, or mallows.
 	
GONZALO
    And were the king on 't, what would I do?
 	
SEBASTIAN
    'Scape being drunk, for want of wine.
	What does the word "plantation" suggest about how Gonzalo sees his ideal state?

GONZALO
    I' the commonwealth I would by contraries
    Execute all things, for no kind of traffic
    Would I admit; no name of magistrate;
    Letters should not be known; riches, poverty,
    And use of service, none; contract, succession,
    Bourn, bound of land, tilth, vineyard, none;
    No use of metal, corn, or wine, or oil;
    No occupation; all men idle, all;
    And women too, but innocent and pure;
    No sovereignty;--
 	
SEBASTIAN
    Yet he would be king on 't.
	What does this list suggest is the ideal state?
	
	Is there anything that Gonzalo feels is good about how things currently are?

ANTONIO
    The latter end of his commonwealth forgets the beginning.
 	
GONZALO
    All things in common nature should produce,
    Without sweat or endeavour: treason, felony,
    Sword, pike, knife, gun, or need of any engine,
    Would I not have; but nature should bring forth,
    Of its own kind, all foison, all abundance,
    To feed my innocent people.
	Are Antonio and Sebastian justified in their criticism? Explain.

SEBASTIAN
    No marrying 'mong his subjects?
 	
ANTONIO
    None, man; all idle: whores and knaves.
 	
GONZALO
    I would with such perfection govern, sir,
    To excel the golden age.
	What does Gonzalo suggest is the duty of a monarch? Is he right?

EXPLORING THE MURDEROUS PLOTS

Use the questions in the following table to help you compare the main points of the one successful and two abortive attempts to do away with authority. Because your answers can provide the basic structure for an essay on the topic, they should be as comprehensive as possible.

Antonio's deposition of Prospero (Act I Sc II)	Antonio's plot to kill Alonso (Act II Sc I)	Caliban's plot to kill Prospero (Act III Sc II)
Q. Is the person who thinks up the plot the same person who is to carry out the (main) deed? Why might that be?		
Q. Why does the instigator (Antonio / Caliban) want the person in authority (Prospero / Alonso) done away with?		
Q. Who else is involved, and why do they agree to participate?		
Q. Describe the nature and time of the deposition (or intended deposition).		
Q. Do the plots fail? If yes, why and in what way?		

PROSPERO'S "ART"

"My charms crack not, my spirits obey"

Magic is central to *The Tempest* and its main character, Prospero. Without magic, Prospero would not be able to engineer events the way he does. He would have no hope of regaining his throne, and he would possibly be the same as the other courtiers – a ruler caught up in the intrigues of power and court life. Years before the play, magic kept him aloof from the concerns of daily governance, and that separation ultimately led to his deposition; but it is magic that also gave him the necessary tools to exact his vengeance.

Intertwined with the notion of magic is the question of the strength of Prospero's magic – after all, it seems that most of the magic is actually performed by Ariel, who is indebted to Prospero for setting him free. Prospero's magic is more akin to having a genie in a bottle than actually having any supernatural powers of his own. He does have some magical power, though: setting Miranda to sleep (Act I Sc II), charming Ferdinand (also Act I Sc II) and the courtiers (Act V Sc I) into immobility are feats he seems to perform himself – and, of course, it was his magic that set Ariel free in the first place.

Interestingly enough, two major events are wholly beyond Prospero's magical powers and are the result of fate or chance (both explained in Act I Sc II): the first is the stranding of himself and Miranda on the island "by providence divine", and the second is the courtiers sailing nearby "By accident most strange". One could argue that it is precisely these events that are central to the whole story – without them, there is no play! The use of magic, therefore, seems limited. For one, it would seem that Prospero's magic was not powerful enough to allow him and Miranda to go home before the ships passed by. It was strong enough, however, for him to know who was on the ship. In many ways, his magic de-humanises Prospero, making it necessary for him to give it up in order to return to the real, human, world at the end of the play. Magic in *The Tempest* must also be viewed within the context of the time in which it was written. James I was hugely interested in witchcraft and had written a book on the subject, denouncing the practice, as it was associated with demonology and a pact with the devil – a link Shakespeare had already explored in *Macbeth*.

TASK:

List all of the occurrences of magic within *The Tempest* (including any that took place before the start of the play). For each occurrence, identify:

- What takes place that is magical?
- Is it carried out by Prospero, or by one of his agents?
- Was it necessary to use magic, or could the same effect have been achieved through other means?
- Was the magic good or bad for the subject?
- Did the magic achieve the desired outcome?

MAGICIAN AND BARD

Use this worksheet to explore parallels between Prospero and Shakespeare. Write down any evidence you find in the boxes provided. The bottom panel has been left blank for you to add an idea of your own.

Action	How does this apply to Prospero?	How does this relate to Shakespeare?
Watching action from off-stage		
Setting up other characters for "scenes"		
Conjuring up strange worlds		
Being involved in the action he devises		
Staging plays		

SLAVERY AND SERVITUDE
"Caliban has a new master – get a new man!"

When exploring the theme of slavery and servitude, we must bear in mind that when *The Tempest* was written, servants were commonplace, and slavery was a profitable business for England; the abolition of the slave trade wouldn't occur for another 200 years.

The most prominent slave in the play is Caliban, who seems incapable of shaking off servitude, instead celebrating changing his master like freedom. Shakespeare makes us understand that, because true freedom was an unrealistic prospect for Caliban, replacing the cruel Prospero with mild Stephano would have felt like freedom.

Prospero maintains that they need Caliban to carry out chores; but surely a powerful magician such as he would have no need of someone carrying out menial labour – his magic could perform those tasks. When Caliban meets Stephano and Trinculo (themselves servants of Alonso) their automatic reaction is also to try to use Caliban for their own ends. In Act III Sc II, Caliban talks Stephano into defeating Prospero so that Caliban can serve Stephano. Was this actually what Caliban wanted? In Act I Sc II, he claims that the island was his before Prospero arrived. Perhaps he sees Stephano not as a new, kind master, but as a weak master who will be easy to overthrow.

Servitude is where one human serves another but is treated humanely and with respect (as opposed to slavery, where the servant is treated more like an object). It appears in two ways in *The Tempest*: Ferdinand's punishment (or test) of menial labour and Ariel's indebtedness to Prospero.

Although he is happy to be near to Miranda, Ferdinand views his forced labour as a form of slavery, carried out by a "prisoner of war", whereas Prospero views it as a test and therefore closer to servitude (remarkably, he is carrying out the same duties as Caliban is told to do!). Ariel seems bound by some form of contract to serve Prospero, but he is more of a servant than a slave, sharing his master's thoughts and even advising him.

Not only are Ariel and Caliban different in what they represent (e.g. one representing air, the other earth), they are also at opposite ends of the servant / slave spectrum. However, neither seems to have a life of any value outside of his work for Prospero: Ariel disappears when he is released, while we are led to believe that Caliban will live alone on the island once the others have left.

TASKS:
Compare the way that Prospero talks to Ariel and to Caliban in Act I Sc II. What can we tell about their relationships from this?

Does Prospero show any sign of friendship towards Ariel? How about towards Caliban?

In Act III Sc II, Caliban seems unaware of Ariel's presence as the latter puts words into Trinculo's mouth. At no point in the play does Caliban acknowledge that Ariel even exists. Assuming he is unaware of Ariel, how do you think that Caliban would react when he learns of Ariel's existence? You may want to script a "deleted scene" from the play where Prospero introduces Caliban to his airy spirit.

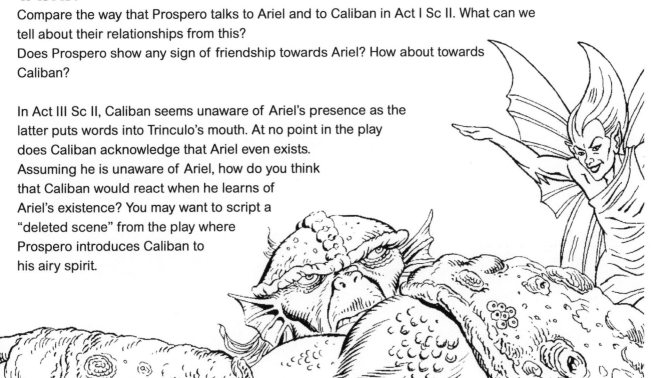

ANALYTICAL ESSAYS

Writing an analytical essay on a theme involves looking at the whole play and discovering how the theme develops, including any build-up and resolution.

To write an analytical essay successfully, it is suggested that pupils use the P-E-E-L structure.
PEEL stands for:

P-oint   Stating the argument.

E-vidence   The evidence for the point, using quotations where applicable.

E-xplain   A deeper explanation of the argument, taking the evidence into account, relative to the theme and the essay title.

L-ink   Reinforce the Point at the end, linking all arguments back to the beginning.

To prepare an essay using this technique, isolate key scenes that deal with the theme and explore each scene with reference to the essay title. These scenes, using quotations where appropriate, will form the backbone of your essay, as they provide the evidence for the arguments.

In order to avoid rambling, it is important that the analysis of the scenes is geared solely towards the title. Similarly, no more than three scenes should be explored in any depth.

The scenes selected do not have to prove the same point - indeed, it is often better to present different views, all of which support (or contradict) the argument, bringing the points together in the conclusion of the essay.

The following worksheets are presented to aid in the preparation of analytical essays:

*   Charting the development of a theme throughout the play;
*   Exploring a theme by briefly analysing a number of key scenes generally (not bound to an essay title);
*   Planning sheet for an analytical essay, including the deeper analysis of three scenes.

EXPLORING HOW THEMES DEVELOP IN THE PLAY

The Tempest is unique among Shakespeare's plays in that it keeps quite closely to the classical unities of time, space and plot. With the exception of Act I Sc I, the whole action takes place on various (almost artificially separated) parts of the island and spans the course of an afternoon – the play almost evolves in real time (centuries before *"24"!*). *The Tempest* also has few confusing sub-plots, making the action quite straightforward.

As this deviation from Shakespeare's norm makes the play more accessible and makes it an ideal candidate for detailed structural analysis. Using the classical division of plays into five acts, pupils can examine how the themes develop as the play progresses.

According to the classical five act model:

> Act I is the exposition. We are introduced to the main characters and themes; the action begins.
>
> Act II is the development. The action introduced in Act I is further developed. Often, sub-plots are introduced at this stage, almost as background noise.
>
> Act III is the climax. The action comes to a head here, resulting in some change in the protagonist. From here, events speed towards their unravelling in the finale.
>
> Act IV is the antithesis of Act II; it is the unravelling of the conflict that came to a head in Act III. Sub-plots are usually resolved to some degree in this act.
>
> Act V is the resolution for good or bad (depending on whether the play is a tragedy or comedy). The action set in motion in Act I is brought to a final conclusion, and the main themes are resolved.

Within this concept it is interesting, for example, to take Act III as the central act and then infer what the play is actually about from the action taking place. Alternatively, you may consider to what extent Act V resolves all issues. Furthermore, although Act I is meant to set the scene, in *The Tempest* it is also used to describe what happened before the play started (in a way, setting the scene of the already established relationships). To analyse the structure and how themes are introduced and developed, pupils could be asked to chart one or more themes through the acts using a graph that visualises the classical structure with a tension line*.

THE STRUCTURE OF *THE TEMPEST*

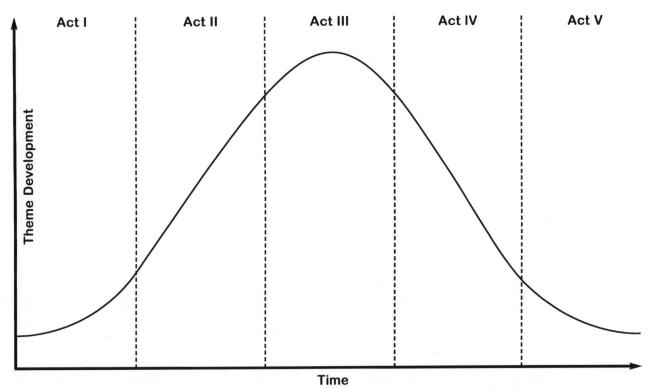

*In completing the graph, the pupils, of course, do not have to stay below the graph line; this is for illustrative purposes only.

THEME EXPLORATION SHEET

Use the following worksheet to help organise your thoughts around the theme of your choice.

THEME:	
Select a scene in which the theme is central	
Summarise the scene briefly, using quotations where appropriate, showing how the theme is present	What does the scene tell us about the theme? Note all observations that are connected to the theme.
Select another scene in which the theme is central or present.	
Summarise the scene briefly, using quotations where appropriate, showing how the theme is present	What does the scene tell us about the theme? Note all observations that are connected to the theme.
If possible, select a third scene in which the theme is central or present.	
Summarise the scene briefly, using quotations where appropriate, showing how the theme is present	What does the scene tell us about the theme? Note all observations that are connected to the theme.
If possible, select a fourth scene in which the theme is central or present.	
Summarise the scene briefly, using quotations where appropriate, showing how the theme is present	What does the scene tell us about the theme? Note all observations that are connected to the theme.

ESSAY WRITING FRAME

Use the framework to help you organise your ideas for an essay on the theme of your choice.

TITLE OF ESSAY (the statement)

First paragraph: Introduction

Briefly discuss the statement. What are the main points? Link the statement to *The Tempest*.

Second paragraph: Illustrate the statement with an example.

Find a passage in the play that can be used as an example for the point you're trying to make.	What does this passage show in relation to the statement?

Third paragraph: illustrate the statement with a second example.

Find a scene in the play that can be used as an example for the point you're trying to make.	What does this passage show in relation to the statement?

Fourth paragraph: Use a third example to illustrate the statement.

Find a part in the play that can be used as an example for the point you're trying to make.	What does this passage show in relation to the statement?

Fifth paragraph: Conclusion – your opinion.

Does the statement hold true or not? Perhaps it is only occasionally true?	Briefly re-cap the main points and finish with your own opinion.

POSSIBLE ESSAY TITLES

A selection of possible essay titles centred around each of the main themes of *The Tempest*.

Legitimate Rule & Social Order

1. What does *The Tempest*, with its multiple plots to depose various rulers, suggest about the nature of power?
2. Was Antonio right to take over government from his brother? Explain your answer in detail.
3. The first scene of the play shows the structure of authority turned around, as the Boatswain orders the king to leave the deck. In what way is this programmatic of the play? Does the entire play show common structures of authority reversed or jeopardised?
4. Two of the plots to depose a ruler revolve around Prospero. Does this suggest he is a bad or inadequate ruler? Explain your answer.
5. What does Gonzalo's description of the perfect state suggest about authority and social order? Try to relate your arguments to the world of *The Tempest* as well as to Shakespeare's time.
6. Based on evidence in *The Tempest*, is monarchy the ideal form of government?
7. Why does Prospero insist so decidedly on Ferdinand and Miranda remaining chaste until their marriage? In what way might that tie in with the theme of legitimate rule?

Magic

1. To what extent is Prospero's magic a tool of his vengeance? Would he be able to exact his revenge without his magic?
2. Prospero's magic sets him apart from the rest of humanity. It is therefore necessary that he gives it up (as he does) before returning to the real world. Discuss.
3. For all his power, Prospero cannot use his magic to bring about any change that really matters. Discuss.
4. All magic is inherently evil insofar as it is contrary to nature. To what extent does this apply to Prospero's magic?
5. Prospero's magic has often been equated with the playwright and director's art. To what extent do you agree with this?

Slavery and Servitude

1. In his occupation of the island, Prospero relies heavily on the services of others. What does this tell us about his character?
2. It can be said that the servants are the true masters in *The Tempest*, and they influence their masters. In what way?
3. To what extent do you think Shakespeare might be criticising slavery in his portrayal of Caliban and Ariel's treatment by Prospero?
4. Caliban is a born slave. Discuss.
5. Prospero forces Ferdinand to work as his servant. How does Ferdinand differ from Caliban?

Betrayal and Forgiveness

1. To what extent is betrayal punished in *The Tempest*?
2. At the end of the play, Prospero forgives Antonio and Alonso. How heartfelt do you think this forgiveness is?
3. An integral part of forgiveness is repentance. To what extent does this apply to the characters in *The Tempest*?
4. The plot of Antonio and Sebastian to kill Alonso never comes to fruition. To what degree do you think Prospero is betraying Alonso by not telling him of the attempt on his life?
5. Is Caliban's plot to do away with Prospero less of a betrayal than the other plots to depose Prospero or Alonso? Explain your answer in detail.

Colonisation

1. Caliban was often depicted as a villain. Is he really evil, or are his actions the justified rebelliousness of a repressed native?
2. The courtiers treat Caliban with nothing but disdain. To what extent does this mirror the Europeans' treatment of Native Americans?
3. *The Tempest* has often been described as an allegory of colonisation. What is meant by this, and to what extent do you agree?
4. The conflict between Caliban and Prospero is based on an incorrect understanding of ownership of land. Discuss.
5. To what extent do you think Shakespeare criticises the colonisation of America?
6. Do you think language is used to suppress Caliban? Explain your answer.

Fate and Justice

1. To what extent do you think it was necessary for Prospero to orchestrate events, or would fate have led to some form of realisation and repentance on Alonso's part without Prospero's intervention?
2. Based on events in *The Tempest,* to what extent do you think we have to pay for our sins in this world?
3. Do you think the characters in *The Tempest* are led by fate, or are the references to fate merely figures of speech? Explain your answer.
4. Is Prospero just? Explain your answer.
5. At the end of the play, Prospero decides to forgive the "three men of sin." Do you think this is the right thing to do? Explain your answer.
6. To what extent do the characters receive their just deserts?

DRAMA ACTIVITIES

Introduction

Because *The Tempest* is a play, any intense involvement with the text – to be successful – must involve acting of some sort. Pupils don't need to act out the whole play or even entire scenes to get a flavour of the piece. Short, focused exercises can help pupils engage with the play as it was intended – namely, acted.

There are a number of general activities that can be used in various circumstances and adapted to suit the focus of the lesson. The most important of these are:

Freeze Framing

A number of pupils are asked to recreate a scene. They are given some time to work out where to position the characters, what expression their faces should show and what gestures to make. Then, when the teacher says, "freeze", they must get into the correct positions and hold the freeze, basically forming a three-dimensional photo (rather like a panel in the graphic novel).

Pupils can be unfrozen a group at a time to give them a chance to look at what other pupils have done. This allows a brief discussion / peer review about what makes a particular freeze effective.

You may wish to extend this technique by allowing frozen characters to briefly describe what their character is thinking.

Hot-Seating

This is a drama activity particularly suited to exploring character and motivation. One pupil is chosen to play the part of a character from the text (e.g. Sebastian), and the rest of the class asks questions, which the pupil has to answer as he believes that character would, in character.

Ideally the questions should be fired quite quickly, much like at a news conference, challenging the hot-seated pupil's thinking and ability to build up a credible character around the information contained in the play.

Repetition of Phrases

A very good way of gauging the effectiveness of language and the pitch of a delivery is to take a short phrase and repeat it in as many different ways as possible, e.g. angrily, joyfully, spitefully, worriedly, doubtfully. This will help the pupils listen to their voices and modulate them according to mood as well as discover which mood suits a certain line best. Recording this in audio only, or even video with audio, provides valuable feedback to the pupil.

Short Interchanges

Similar to extended freeze-frames, this is a great method for some very basic character acting. Pupils are paired up, and each is assigned a character and a small number of lines for an interaction. From those lines, each pupil selects one line that he or she feels best represents the main message from that character. The pupils then say their lines in turn, trying to put as much emphasis as possible into their one selected line, using gestures and facial expressions. In that way, they distill their given character into one line and a gesture. Developments of relationship can also be explored using this technique by choosing lines that follow the play's development.

Short Speech

Asking pupils to prepare a short speech (e.g. Francisco's) is an ideal way of developing speaking skills. Ideally, pupils would memorise the extract so that they can give a good delivery (without a sheet obstructing their connection with the audience). This would also enable them to add more gestures and facial expression to their delivery, deepening their character acting.

It is a great idea to record the pupils as they speak, using video equipment. Playing this back to them and discussing what they did well and what they need to work on, based on the impartial evidence of a recording, is one of the best ways to improve speaking skills.

DRAMA ACTIVITIES

More advanced techniques include:

Mime

One of the great difficulties pupils experience is how to act without talking, how to behave when on stage but not actually delivering any lines. Exercises that involve mime are a great way to help overcome this difficulty. It is possible to mime simple emotions or to act out a whole scene without saying a word – or with the teacher or a pupil reading the lines and all the pupils acting along without saying a word.

Improvisation

This technique requires courage and a detailed knowledge of the characters. It is therefore best combined with character work. The technique involves putting the characters into a scene that is not in the play (e.g. the first meeting of Prospero and Ariel) and asking them to act the scene out straight away, with no preparation. Harrowing as this experience can be for some pupils, it encourages quick thinking, staying in role and character study.

Some ideas for activities involving drama techniques include:

- Hot-seat Prospero after Act I Scene II. Questions should revolve around his deposition, whether he thinks it fair, or why it came about, why he didn't play a more active role, etc.
- Hot-seat Gonzalo after his "commonwealth" speech. Questions should revolve around his concept of the ideal state, how it might be put into practice (many have tried throughout history), why he would be a fit ruler, how he would guard against corruption, and similar issues. Questions could be mocking, much like Sebastian's and Antonio's broadsides.
- Hot-seat Antonio, Sebastian and Alonso after they have returned to Milan. Questions should revolve around whether they feel remorse, whether their stay on the island has changed them in any way and what they think about Prospero reappearing and forgiving them.
- Select a number of opposing characters (Prospero – Caliban, Gonzalo – Antonio) or characters in dialogue (Miranda – Ferdinand, Ariel – Prospero) and give each character only one line to say. Split the class in half and assign a character to each side. Pupils must say their one line emphatically, with one gesture.
- Francisco has only one short speech in the whole play. This makes it ideal as a test-piece, as his entire character must be inferred from these few lines. Ask pupils to prepare a delivery of the speech. They can coach each other in pairs before delivering their performance to the class.
- Freeze-frame the various moments of betrayal (see page 58) and, while in freeze, say one thought each character might have. Analyse how the moments are different and what they have in common.
- Freeze-frame the ten most important scenes. Pupils can either make up individual lists of ten, or the list can be drawn up together in class (better, because this allows for a comparison of freezes). Freeze all ten moments in succession, keeping the best freeze each time for other pupils to see and then (when unfrozen) to comment on their effectiveness.
- Imagine a dialogue between Caliban and Ariel about Prospero. They're each revealing what they think of him and how he treats them. What might each one say? The dialogue could take place after Prospero has left the island. If pupils feel confident enough, this dialogue could be improvised.

TEN LINES IN THE LIMELIGHT

Francisco's Speech

Francisco only has ten lines in the play (technically only nine, as two are half-lines). Any actor playing Francisco therefore only has those ten lines (barring miming throughout various scenes) to effectively bring across his entire character. Because everything we can know about Francisco's character is contained within those ten lines (no other character talks to him), it is an ideal speech to focus on. So, what makes a delivery effective? How can Francisco best be brought to life?

1. Focus on the passage. What does it tell us about Francisco? What can we deduce about the kind of person he is from what he says?
   From his speech we can gain clues about Francisco's traits, age and background.
2. Focus on the words that precede his speech. Why does Francisco talk when he does? How does Francisco interact with the other characters? With whom does he interact?
3. Flesh him out. Based on what you have discovered so far and on the whole play, give Francisco a credible background. You should deduce things like why he was on the ship, what his position at court is, and who his friends are. Again, you may have to make this up, but it must be in keeping with the play.

Bear all this in mind when practicing the speech and let it help form the way you deliver the lines. When rehearsing the speech, also bear in mind the following:

- Vary the volume and pitch of your voice. Nothing is duller than a flat, monotonous rendition; but be careful not to overdo it, as this will sound artificial.
- Add an emotional edge to your voice, where appropriate
- Even though the text is written in one long block, remember you can (and should!) pause wherever you feel it is appropriate. You could even repeat some of the words, if this makes your delivery more captivating.
- Use gestures to underline important words or emotions.
- Think how you talk and let that influence your delivery – it will make your speech appear more natural.

Of course, all of this applies to any given character you perform.

CHARACTERISTIC ONE-LINERS
"A word, good sir"

Below is a selection of one-liners that – in juxtaposition – can be used to explore character and how to show personality when acting.

PROSPERO: Thou didst seek to violate the honour of my child	**CALIBAN:** Oh ho, oh ho! Would 't had been done!
PROSPERO: Hag-seed, hence! Fetch us in fuel	**CALIBAN:** I must obey: his art is of such power, it would control my dam's god
FERDINAND: O you, so perfect and so peerless, are created of every creature's best!	**MIRANDA:** I would not wish any companion in the world but you
GONZALO: How lush and lusty the grass looks! How green!	**ANTONIO:** The ground, indeed, is tawny
SEBASTIAN: Draw thy sword: one stroke shall free thee from the tribute which thou pay'st	**ANTONIO:** Draw together; and when I rear my hand, do you the like
STEPHANO: Trinculo, keep a good tongue in your head	**TRINCULO:** I did not give the lie. Out o' your wits, and hearing too?

CHARACTERISTIC ONE-LINERS
"Soft, sir! One word more."

This exercise can also be used to chart how a relationship develops between two characters. The following one-liners trace the relationship between Prospero and Ariel.

PROSPERO: Approach, my Ariel, come!	ARIEL: All hail, great master! grave sir, hail!
ARIEL: Is there more toil? Since thou dost give me pains, Let me remember thee what thou hast promis'd	PROSPERO: How now? Moody? What is 't thou canst demand?
PROSPERO: After two days I will discharge thee.	ARIEL: That's my noble master! What shall I do?
ARIEL: Thy thoughts I cleave to. What's thy pleasure?	PROSPERO: Spirit, we must prepare to meet Caliban
PROSPERO: Hey, Mountain, hey!	ARIEL: Silver! there it goes, Silver!
ARIEL: If you now beheld them, your affections would become tender.	PROSPERO: Dost thou think so, spirit?
ARIEL: Was 't well done?	PROSPERO: Bravely, my diligence! Thou shalt be free.

TASK:
Create a similar chart of one-liners that best capture the relationship between one or more of the following:

- Ferdinand and Miranda
- Stephano and Trinculo
- Prospero and Caliban

ACTING OUT SCENES FROM THE PLAY
"These our actors, as I foretold you, were all spirits"

Acting out scenes in class is always a challenge – in a variety of ways. Discipline can be an issue (especially as excitement mounts), so it is important to establish clear rules and procedures for when pupils need to pay attention. The greatest problems will probably be the amount of space and involving all pupils. The opening and closing scenes of *The Tempest* are particularly suited to being acted out in class. Both scenes can be staged in a way that involves all pupils, and both present a challenge, but in different ways: the opening scene must be exciting and involve the audience, which means staging as realistic a storm as possible – not an easy task; as Prospero talks to various characters in the final scene and forgives them, there is an ever-increasing number of actors on the stage with no lines, which means that pupils must mime long stretches – again, not simple to do.

Act I Scene I:
The main factors that need to be borne in mind here are a convincing representation of the storm, with wind and waves. Those with speaking parts need to represent the urgency of the situation and not just speak their lines. Pauses, repetitions and raising the voice will be important techniques to ensure a credible delivery in this scene.
Some ideas on how to represent the storm:
- A large blue blanket could be used to represent the sea. Pupils holding the edges could flap it up and down while emulating the sound the wind or the water might make
- Have some pupils dress in blue (jeans and a blue T- or sweatshirt) and let them be the waves that beat against the ship, break over the deck, possibly even tearing mariners with them, until they consume the ship.
- All mariners and courtiers could sway from side to side as they come on stage to mimic the motion of the ship. For this to be really effective, the swaying should be synchronised.
- The deck could be raised above the stage level, to make the jumping off the sinking ship more dramatic. Blue mats on the floor would not only break the fall, but also emulate the blue of the sea.
- Make use of the music department to find percussion instruments that can simulate a storm (drums, cymbals etc.). Lighting will be more difficult, but darkening the room and using torches with a flash function is a possibility.

Act V Scene I (excerpts):
This is difficult to stage, as actors enter the scene as it progresses and all are united in front of Prospero. In addition, the dialogue is quite structured and staid, with one party expressing its amazement and Prospero answering. Until Stephano and Trinculo arrive, for example, Sebastian only says one line, and Antonio is silent – what do they do the whole time?
To make the structure easier, acting could focus on lines 62-87, 104-135, 165-196 and 256-294 although teachers may wish to include the part where the Boatswain and the Master arrive as this is an occasion to include more pupils.
Some ideas on how to stage the characters:
- Group similar characters together – so Gonzalo and Alonso would be talking to one another, as would Sebastian and Antonio. However, it could be interesting to invert this and have Antonio try to persuade Alonso that this is all just a fantasy and Sebastian make fun of the all-too-credulous Gonzalo.
- Antonio and Sebastian must fear Prospero after the revelation that he knows about their plot to kill Alonso – how do they react? Are they plotting to kill both Alonso and Prospero when the opportunity arises, or do they think they've met their match? Do both react the same way?
- Where are Miranda and Ferdinand as they are revealed? When and how do they become aware of the fact that they are being watched?
- To what extent are Stephano, Trinculo and Caliban still drunk or just hurt and hung-over? They are obviously aching from having been chased, so they should limp – can they walk far? Do they just enter and break down, mirroring how Stephano found Trinculo and Caliban?

These are only suggestions for how to act out two scenes, but any scene can be adapted for acting out in the classroom. The more time and effort you put into a "mini-production", the more rewarding it will be and the more the pupils will gain from the experience of exploring play scripts for themselves and bringing their own personal slant to a text.
The step from acting in class to production is a big one, however, and many more things need to be considered to do this. Some of the issues of staging (as opposed to acting) are explored in the chapter on Stagecraft (page 88).

CHARACTERS ON TRIAL

"Though with their high wrongs I am struck to the quick"

An exciting way to resolve open issues through the use of dramatic techniques is to put a character on trial. Due to the vast amount of betrayals and occupations of the island, practically every character in *The Tempest* can be put on trial to answer for their actions. Some ideas are:

- Put Alonso, Sebastian and Antonio on trial for their crimes (as Prospero does in the play). Prospero would prosecute, and either Ariel or fate could be the judge, with pupils being the jury.
- Prospero could be put on trial for his alleged theft of the island from Caliban.
- Caliban could be tried for inciting Stephano and Trinculo to murder Prospero.

Whenever staging a court scene, it is important that there are court officials as well as the characters from the play who are either witnesses or prosecuting. The officials are:

- A judge
- A jury of at least five with a single leader
- A prosecutor (which can be one of the characters from the play)
- A defence lawyer

A number of pupils can take on the roles of prosecution and defence, alternating their speeches and questions, if necessary, to ensure all pupils are involved.

All pupils must adhere to protocol, which must be agreed on and understood in advance. Although this may appear to hamper the flow at first, strict protocol actually makes the proceedings easier to stage and follow. Because of the importance of protocol, it is advisable to have the teacher as (non-deciding) judge for the first few times this activity is carried out.

It is equally important to set out the classroom so that it physically resembles a court.

Pupils should be given time to prepare opening and closing speeches. Ideally these should be timed or an approximate timeframe given. Arguments and evidence should be based on the text and not made up. Ultimately, it will be the jury who decides the case. Pupils who are members of the jury should therefore take notes and give careful consideration to all aspects of the case. It is the job of the leader of the jury to make sure the jury reaches a verdict, such as by leading the deliberation and asking relevant questions of the jury members concerning the crime for which the accused is being tried.

CRIMINAL PROCEEDINGS
RULES OF PROCEDURE

Layout of court:

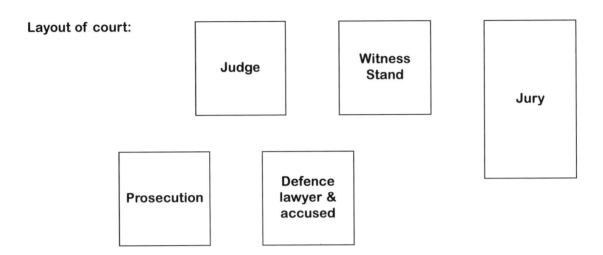

1. The judge opens the proceedings by stating the case (e.g. "The case of the crown against [name] for alleged [crime]")

2. The prosecution opens with a brief statement, immediately followed by the same from the defence lawyer. The judge then asks the accused how he or she pleads ("guilty" or "not guilty").

3. Proceedings start with the examination of the accused by the prosecution, followed by questions from the defence.

4. The prosecution calls in its witnesses, one by one. The judge asks each one to swear an oath of truth, then hands questioning over to the prosecution. When the prosecution has no more questions to ask a witness, the defence has a chance to ask questions to establish certain facts or undermine credibility.

5. After all prosecution witnesses have been heard, the defence calls in and questions its witnesses. As with Step 4, once the defence has finished with each witness, the prosecution questions and challenges them.

6. The party not questioning can raise any objection if they think the questioner is being unfair, is leading the witness, or is making irrelevant statements. The party simply says "Objection" with a short reason and the judge then decides whether it is "Granted" or "Denied". The judge does not have to give reasons but must aim to be fair. If an objection is granted, the questioner is not allowed to continue the question; any objectionable evidence given must be disregarded by the jury.

7. When there are no more witnesses, the parties make their final pleas, starting with the prosecution lawyer, then the defence.

8. The jury deliberates in private (but in class this can be public to ensure a good discussion) and then gives its verdict in writing to the judge (delivered to the judge by the leader of the jury).

9. The judge passes judgement on the accused according to the verdict of the jury and sets the punishment.

DEBATING ISSUES
RULES OF PROCEDURE

Layout of room:

Proposition	Chairperson/	Opposition
1st speaker	Timekeeper	1st speaker
2nd speaker		2nd speaker
(3rd speaker)		(3rd speaker)

Floor

1. The Proposition is the side in favour of a motion, the Opposition the side against it. Depending on the number of pupils and the time available, you can choose to have two or three speakers on each team. A debate with two speakers should take about 30 minutes, one with three about 45 minutes.

2. The Chairperson and Timekeeper can be the same person, but it is easier for the chair if they are separate. The job of the Chairperson is to welcome the speakers, announce the topic, and then ensure that the debate is carried out according to the rules of procedure.

3. The order of speeches is: 1st speaker Proposition – 1st speaker Opposition – 2nd speaker Proposition – 2nd speaker Opposition – 3rd speaker Proposition – 3rd speaker Opposition (if you have three speakers).

4. Each speech should be two minutes long. Of these two minutes, the first and last 30 seconds are protected, meaning the speaker may not be interrupted. After 30 seconds, the Timekeeper gives a signal to indicate that speakers from the opposing team may stand up and say "Point of information" (PoI), meaning they have a question or remark to make. The speaker may accept or decline the PoI. If the PoI is accepted, the questioner makes his statement and then sits down again. The speaker can choose whether or not to react to the PoI. After 1 minute 30 seconds, another signal is given to show that the time for PoI is over.

5. After all speakers have spoken, the floor (the audience) is invited to ask questions. Questioners should stand when they speak and address the question to a specific person. The addressee also stands. Both remain standing until the question has been answered.

6. After the floor discussion, which can take as long as the chairman sees fit, the 1st speaker of the Opposition makes a summary speech, briefly re-capping the main points of the Opposition's arguments and taking the floor discussion into account. After that, the 1st speaker of the Proposition gives his or her summary speech. Both summary speeches should be around two minutes long and are fully protected (i.e. no questions or interruptions).

7. After the summary speeches, the Chairman asks the floor to vote on the motion. The Chairman counts the votes, declares the winner and closes the debate.

The English-Speaking Union (www.esu.org) has some great resources and know-how on public speaking and debating.

STAGECRAFT – INTRODUCTION

"I must bestow upon the eyes... some vanity of mine art"

It is one thing to act out scenes in class in order to explore character and the different ways of delivering lines (as well as developing speaking and listening skills); actually staging a performance of parts or all of a play is another thing entirely! The term "stagecraft" describes this difference, and it involves such things as props, costumes and scenery, as well as envisioning scenes and directorial issues, like training and coaching actors to deliver the vision that the director wants to create.

The various areas cannot be clearly divided; for example, they are all influenced by directorial decisions, while scenery and costume must link to create a convincing and organic performance experience. Nevertheless, the following activities have been separated according to where the main focus lies, to aid the presentation of this difficult aspect of theatre.

Stage and Scenery:

The scenery is one of the most important visual stimuli for an audience. It helps to create the atmosphere and transports them into the world of the play. There is a wide range of possibilities, from a naturalistic portrayal of the surroundings to a bare stage, with possibly only colour-coding or light effects. When devising scenery, it is important not only to know what one wants to depict and how realistic one wants it to be, but also the mood to be recreated and how this can be achieved (e.g. through the use of lighting and colour).

In the context of the reconstructed Jacobean Globe Theatre in London, work could revolve around recreating scenery for this historical open-air theatre, making use of the stage area, the balconies and the pillars.

Some ideas for work on stage and scenery are:

- Act I Scene I is one of the few challenging scenes to produce, as it involves a storm and a shipwreck: things that are difficult to actually show on stage. Pupils are to think about how they would stage this scene and then to draw a detailed stage plan with props and scenery, explaining their choices. Other scenes which might challenge the inventiveness of the pupils are Act III Scene III, with the disappearing banquet and Ariel as harpy, and Act IV Scene I with the masque and goddesses flying in from the heavens.
- Using the sketch of the stage at The Globe on the following page, pupils are to choose a scene from the play and set it on the Jacobean stage (or its modern equivalent). They could also add cut-out drawings of characters in costume and quotations (in speech bubbles) to make a whole scene come to life. Pupils should be encouraged to explain their choice of scene, scenery and costume.
- Pupils could be asked to draw sketches of scenery for each scene of the play. As a particular challenge, they could try to have one scene that fits all five acts, with just a number of props highlighting the differences. They should draw the scene(s) and any props they would need.
- Focusing on props, pupils could be asked to design Prospero's wand, his magic books, the wood that Caliban and Ferdinand have to carry, the table with the feast on it or any other relevant object that might be used in the staging of the play.

Costume:

Particularly in modern productions with sparser scenery, costumes are a prime marker for setting and atmosphere. As the most visible object directly pertaining to the characters and fused to them (so to speak), they are also important pointers of traits. As such, they greatly influence the audience's view of a character. A "darker" clothed Prospero and a "lighter" clothed Caliban say a lot about the approach a director has chosen. Costumes thus, possibly even more than scenery, send out clear signals and messages about the play's interpretation and characterisation.

Some ideas for work on costumes are:

- Ask pupils to design a costume for Prospero. There should be two designs – one with Prospero wearing his cloak and holding his staff, the other his "normal" appearance, i.e. when not wearing the cloak.
- Caliban has been portrayed in a number of various guises. To what degree is he a monster? To what extent a man? Pupils should draw how they envisage Caliban, making sure it is a costume that an actor could wear and move around in.
- Discuss how you could make it clear that Antonio is evil. What costume and make-up would you use? Pupils could also discuss whether to make it obvious or more subtle that Antonio was a "baddie".
- When pupils have produced a costume design (creating a cross-curricular link with Art), the teacher could ask other pupils to comment on what they can infer about the character based solely on the costume design.

THE GLOBE STAGE

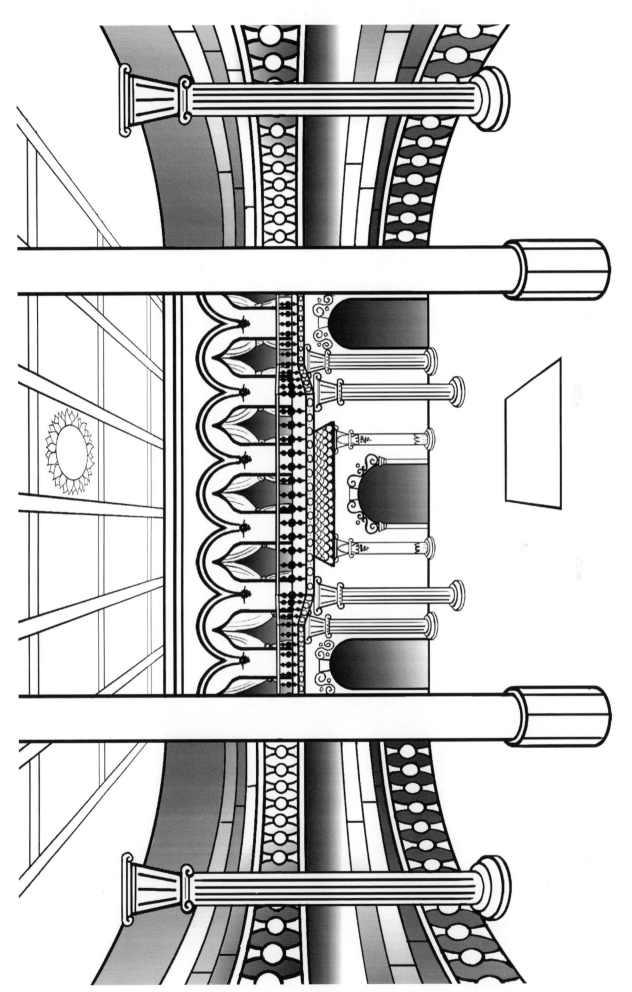

COSTUME DESIGN

"By this hand, I'll have that gown"

Use the outline on this page to help you create a costume for one of the characters in *The Tempest*.

Name of Character: _____

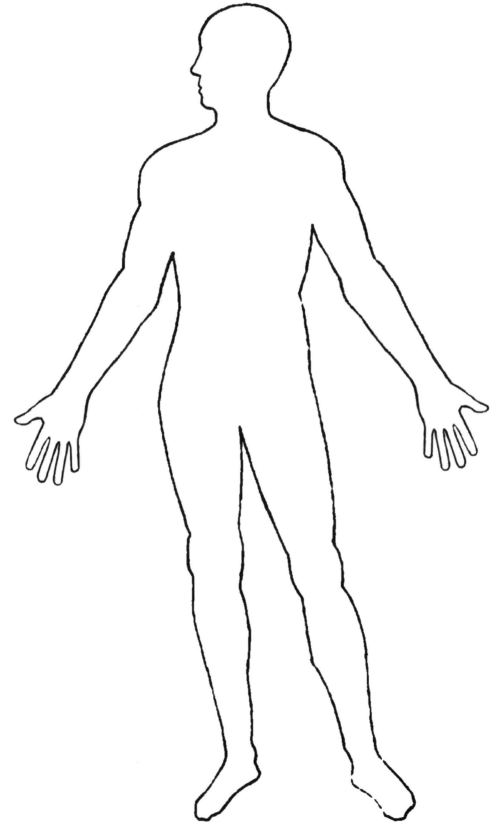

STORYBOARDING

Storyboarding:

This technique comes from the film industry and is very much like creating a comic book version of a scene, but the frames cover a much shorter space of time. The idea of a storyboard is to show, by using drawings, every different shot the viewers of a film will see. In this respect, it is a guide to the production crew and director.

For class work, its strength lies in the focus of attention it allows. Because it moves more slowly than a comic, a frame does not have to contain any text and so can contain any number of spoken lines. Storyboarding, by directing the view of the reader, allows a level of focus that a theatre performance cannot give. For a particular emotional impact, pupils might want to focus on the eyes or the mouth only. Drawing skills, although handy, are not necessary; it must only be clear what each frame is showing. Notes can make up for deficits in draughtsmanship.

Storyboarding is particularly suited to scenes of high emotional intensity or where there is a lot of action. Some ideas for scenes are:

- Storyboard the discovery of Caliban and Trinculo by Stephano in Act II Scene II. The aim should be to bring out the comic nature of this scene.
- The ending of the play demands a strong delivery by Prospero. How might a film emphasise this? Pupils are to explore this issue using storyboards, trying to capture the earnestness of Prospero's plea as well as his helplessness without his magic.
- Based on a storyboard, some pupils could act out a scene while other pupils film them, making sure the image and view selected on the recording matches the storyboard's views and angles.

(There is a blank storyboard sheet on page 92).

Directorial Issues:

All decisions concerning how to act certain parts, which setting or thematic background to give the play, and how to interpret the characters, are ultimately the director's choice. Any production of *The Tempest* (or any play, for that matter) is a result of a director's vision and ideas. Directorial work is therefore very broad and encompasses all forms of stagecraft. A director may delegate work to other parties (such as costume design), but in the end it is he or she who makes the final decision on all aspects.

Some ideas for work on directorial issues are:

- Make a short film of the epilogue (it is advisable to storyboard this prior to filming).
- What is the most important part of the play? Pupils should think about what they think is the crux, explain why this is, and consider how they would gear a performance to best show this central idea.
- What alternatives are there for a setting? What modern-day equivalent to the themes can the pupils find (e.g. businessmen trading with an exploited, lesser-developed country)? They should write down ideas for scenery and costumes and how to interpret each role.
- Write notes to help the actor of Prospero, Caliban or Ariel understand his (or her) role – how should the part be acted? What history of the character (his "back story") should the actor bear in mind? What kind of a person is that character?
- Where would you like to stage the play? – in The Globe, a modern theatre, or outside? Explain your choice.

STORYBOARDING

Use the following frames to help you storyboard your scene.

THE TEMPEST WORD SEARCH

The following words are hidden in the grid below. Words can be horizontal (left to right), vertical (top to bottom) or diagonal (top left to bottom right, or bottom left to top right).

SEBASTIAN	MILAN	NAPLES
PROSPERO	SPIRIT	GONZALO
KING	DUKE	FERDINAND
SERVANT	SETEBOS	BERMUDA
MIRANDA	TRINCULO	ARIEL
DIDO	ALGIERS	FRANCISCO
BOATSWAIN	CALIBAN	TUNIS

```
A  O  F  R  A  N  C  I  S  C  O  M  S  W
G  O  N  Z  A  L  O  B  E  R  M  U  D  A
I  T  A  R  I  E  L  O  R  D  I  D  O  O
P  N  K  T  S  E  B  A  S  T  I  A  N  T
P  O  A  I  I  E  L  T  U  N  I  S  T  A
R  R  I  P  N  E  I  S  N  I  N  B  R  D
O  F  M  M  L  G  G  W  A  A  R  E  I  E
S  E  I  I  E  N  A  B  S  K  S  N  S
P  R  R  R  S  T  S  I  T  U  O  S  C  A
E  D  A  A  P  A  L  N  D  B  R  P  U  R
R  I  N  N  I  A  A  M  E  E  M  I  L  S
O  N  A  D  C  V  G  T  I  P  I  R  O  I
M  A  I  A  R  A  E  G  E  L  L  I  K  I
B  N  B  E  T  S  L  E  A  T  A  T  I  A
M  D  S  O  C  A  G  I  A  A  N  A  N  I
```

THE TEMPEST WORD SEARCH

The following words are hidden in the grid below. They may be forwards, backwards, horizontal, vertical or diagonal. How many times does each word appear?

LIQUOR ( )	TREACHEROUS ( )	GARMENT ( )	VENGEANCE ( )
PREROGATIVE ( )	APPARITION ( )	PLANTATION ( )	CONFIDENCE ( )
INVETERATE ( )	MARKETABLE ( )	AFFLICTION ( )	GRUMBLINGS ( )
VILLAINOUS ( )	INSUBSTANTIAL ( )	FATHOMS ( )	USURP ( )
IMPOSTER ( )	DESTINY ( )	THUNDERCLAPS ( )	DILIGENCE ( )
LANGUAGE ( )	HARPY ( )	BETRAYAL ( )	PERFIDIOUS ( )

```
L M I F I N S U B S T A N T I A L A Y A R T E B P U
A S N T A H R Y P R A H A C S N F I M P O S T I R E
N U N O R O A B E L M E V I L L A E N O U S N N U D
G O E P I E R R O A A E E L B A T E K R A M N C S T
U N G Y N T A E P T D N E L A V H E H A R P Y U U I
A I A R P T C C T Y I E T P D C O N F I D E N C E E
G A U E L R H I H S N P S A L I M E E S U S U R P A
E L G A G N A U L E O A R T T A S Y N I S E D N I R
A L N U V A F H N F R P C U I I N S O I D I F R E P
O I A A R E U E N D F O M N S N O T L A Y A R T I B
H V L R T E N G T L E A U I U U Y N A L I Q U O R Y
A Y E I A L E G N H S R H S O R N O E T I R A P P A
R R A T U E O T E A O N C N N I A F F L I C T I O N
P A P U A E L N M A L M O L I F A T H F T O F N O O
Y H P C G R I O R N N N S M A D E S T I N Y N I R L
S N A P O T E I A C I C N I L P D I L I G E N C E P
U V R S A N U T G G L Y E L L P S D E S T I N Y A T
O E I M U F F C E M B R P M I E V I T A G O R E R P
I N T E T P F I L V D R P R V N G F E A A S F R Q P
D G I E T D N L D N N A G I A D K R E G G K O A A G
I E O V F I N F I E A I H O U H P M U N I U U R A L
F A N I M N G F N C N L I Q U O R L I M Q L S S T R
R N I T A T N A L P T C E U T A A L I I B G I N U E
E C I A R O U Q I L U I E H G I B E L A R L C D O I
P E M G A F F L I C T I O N T M P E R F I D I O U S
I M P O S T E R D A N A P N U T N I M R A G A N T A
L P O R Y N I T S E D N A R P L A N T A T I O N G A
G E S E E A F F L I C T G A C O N F I D E N C E I S
P A T R F R E O I A S U O R E H C A E R T I R I T T
R R A P C E O G R B E C N A E G N E V L I Q U O R U
U S U R I N B G U I P R E R O G A T I V E I N M H M
N U T S F A T S A A C S U O I D I F R E P P E Y B N
P T E H U L N R P T G N T T S U O I D I F R E P O R
E C N E D I F N O C I N S U B S T A N T I A L R U E
F N E C N A E G N E V V A P L A N T A T I O N A Q A
P R E R O G A T I V E N E L V E N G E A N C E H I T
P A M E S C H E T O N F Q N N N M A U S R T F V L E
```

94

WHO AM I?

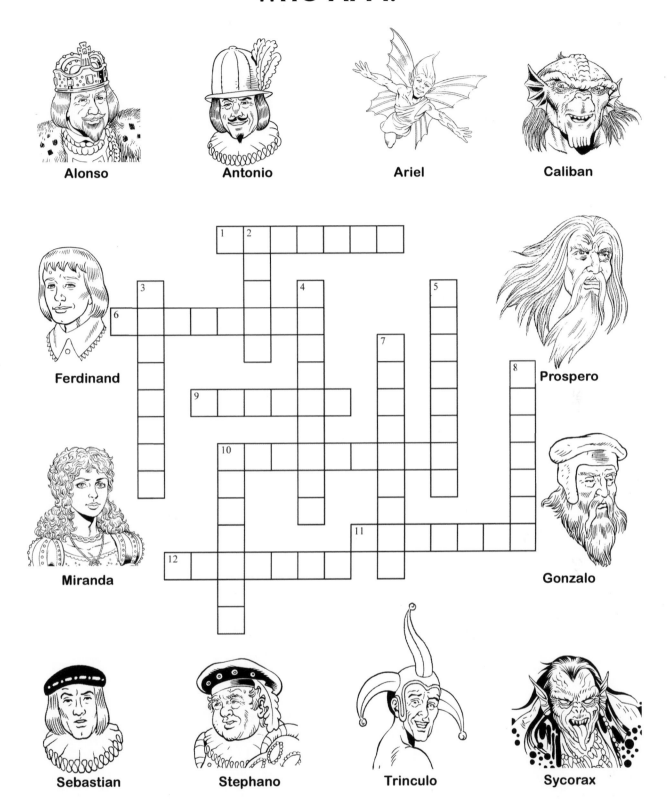

Alonso

Antonio

Ariel

Caliban

Ferdinand

Prospero

Miranda

Gonzalo

Sebastian

Stephano

Trinculo

Sycorax

ACROSS

1 I was born on the island (7)

6 Before I was ousted, I used to be Duke of Milan (8)

9 I'm the King of Naples (6)

10 My brother is the King of Naples (9)

11 I ousted my brother to become Duke of Milan (7)

12 I grew up on the island and was taught by my father, who has magical powers (7)

DOWN

2 I am an airy spirit (5)

3 I am a jester to the King of Naples (8)

4 I tell the King and his courtiers to get below deck during the storm (9)

5 I am a butler to the King of Naples (8)

7 My father is King of Naples (9)

8 I am an advisor to the King of Naples (7)

10 I am a witch who gave birth on the island (7)

Solution (page 12)

THE GLOBE
TEACHERS' VERSION

GLOBE THEATRE: Label Descriptions

The Musician's Gallery
Sometimes live music was played here, but it was also used for acting as a wall or balcony.

The Lord's Rooms
Here was the best place to sit if you were a lord or lady because everyone could see you – but your view might not be very good!

The Tiring House
An area behind the stage where costumes and props were kept and where actors changed.

The Pillars
There were trunks of oak trees put here to hold up The Heavens. The theatre was meant to be like the universe – divided into Heaven, Earth and Hell.

The Heavens
The canopy over the stage, decorated with signs of the zodiac. There was a space above here from which actors could be lowered through a trapdoor as gods or angels.

The Gentlemen's Rooms
Rich playgoers could sit here on cushioned seats.

The Trapdoor
This led down to Hell! It was a room below the stage from where actors playing ghosts, witches and devils could make their entrance.

The Yard
A thousand "groundlings" would stand here to watch the plays. Noisy and smelly!

COMPREHENSION TESTS
TEACHERS' VERSION

Solution (pages 16/17)

Act I

On returning home from __Tunis__, the King of Naples and his courtiers are caught in a __tempest__ close to an __island__. The ship __breaks__, and all seems lost.

On the island, Miranda begs her __father__, __Prospero__, to make sure that no one is hurt in the storm. Prospero reassures her and tells her about their past: __twelve__ years ago, Prospero was Duke of __Milan__. He allowed his __brother__, __Antonio__, to govern instead of him, as he preferred to spend his time in __study__. Eventually, with the help of Alonso, the King of __Naples__, Antonio deposed his brother and set him, together with __Miranda__, adrift in a small boat. They reached the island onto which Antonio, Alonso and the royal __entourage__ are now wrecked. Having put Miranda to sleep, Prospero calls on Ariel, his servant __spirit__. Ariel wants his freedom, but Prospero reminds him how indebted he is to Prospero for rescuing him from a __pine tree__. Ariel flies off to carry out Prospero's orders, while the latter wakes Miranda.

Prospero and Miranda visit Caliban, a __brutish__ servant, whom Prospero claims he treated kindly until Caliban tried to __rape__ Miranda. Caliban is sent off to fetch wood.

Ariel brings Ferdinand, the son of __Alonso__, to Prospero and Miranda. The two young people __fall in love__ at first sight, but Prospero takes Ferdinand __prisoner__, claiming he is a __spy__.

Act II

Alonso is distraught over the loss of his __son__ and __heir__, __Ferdinand__. Nothing __Gonzalo__ says can cheer him up, not even his musings about what he would do, were he __king__ of the island. Alonso feels he has lost his __daughter__, too, as she has just been married to the King of Tunis. Typically (and very unsympathetically) __Sebastian__ says Alonso only has __himself__ to blame for that.

__Ariel__ casts a sleep spell over the courtiers, with the exception of Antonio and Sebastian. Antonio suggests to Sebastian that they kill __Alonso__ and Gonzalo, which would make Sebastian King of Naples, in much the same way that __Antonio__ became Duke of Milan. Just as the two are about to strike, Ariel wakes Gonzalo, who in turn wakes the king. The two plotters make up a swift __lie__ about why their swords are drawn, and they all leave to go in search of Ferdinand.

Elsewhere on the island, Caliban is fetching wood for Prospero. Caliban is scared of his master and hides underneath his __cloak__ when he sees what he believes to be a __spirit__ approaching. It is __Trinculo__, who takes refuge under the same gabardine to escape the approaching __storm__. When __Stephano__ arrives, he is amazed to see the strange __creature__ with four legs and two heads. He gives the monster drink, and Trinculo, realising that it is Stephano, greets his friend. __Caliban__ promises to be a loyal servant to Stephano.

Act III

Ferdinand has to do work for __Prospero__, but he is happy to do it as long as it allows him to be close to __Miranda__. They decide to __marry__, which pleases Prospero, who has been __eavesdropping__ on their conversation. Ariel goes to Stephano, Trinculo and Caliban, and copies __Trinculo__'s voice, thus sowing discord among the three drunkards. Caliban tells __Stephano__ of how Prospero made him his slave, and persuades Stephano to kill Prospero in order to become king of the island, taking Miranda as his __wife__. Ariel overhears the murderous plot and rushes off to tell Prospero.

Alonso and the __courtiers__ are tired from searching for __Ferdinand__. Exhausted, they see __spirits__ laying out a feast. They are __famished__, and they decide to __eat__. However, it is Prospero who conjured up the feast, and just as __Alonso__ approaches the food, it disappears. __Ariel__ reappears, transformed into a frightening __harpy__. In this guise, he tells Alonso that Ferdinand was __drowned__ as punishment to Alonso for him helping to __depose__ Prospero. The king is filled with remorse, but __Antonio__ and Sebastian are __unrepentant__.

COMPREHENSION TESTS
TEACHERS' VERSION

Solution (page 18)

Act IV

Having tested Ferdinand's love, Prospero agrees to let him __**marry**__ Miranda. He makes **Ferdinand** promise not to __**sleep**__ with Miranda until their wedding night. To celebrate their impending __**wedding**__, Prospero has __**spirits**__ perform a masque, in which __**Greek**__ goddesses __**praise**__ marital love and chastity, and bless the happy couple. The masque ends suddenly when __**Prospero**__ remembers __**Caliban**__'s plot to __**kill**__ him.

__**Ariel**__ reports that he has led the three plotters astray and left them in a smelly __**bog**__. Prospero prepares a further __**trap**__. Arriving at Prospero's __**cell**__, Stephano, Trinculo and Caliban are despondent. They discover some fancy __**clothes**__, and **Stephano** and Trinculo try them on. Caliban tries to remind them of their purpose, but his words are in vain. Prospero conjures up some spirits as **hunting dogs** to chase and __**punish**__ all three of them.

Act V

Prospero promises Ariel that he will soon be free. __**Ariel**__ reports the events of the **afternoon**. He has managed to bring all __**parties**__ near to Prospero's cell. Ariel encourages Prospero to __**forgive**__ his brother and __**Alonso**__. The courtiers arrive at the __**cell**__, and Prospero charms them all. He __**forgives**__ each one separately, then puts on the __**clothes**__ he wore when he was Duke of Milan. All are __**surprised**__ to see him again. Alonso wonders how he managed to arrive on **the island**, but Antonio and **Sebastian** still do not seem to __**repent**__. Prospero reveals Ferdinand and Miranda to Alonso and the courtiers. Overjoyed to see his son alive, Alonso agrees to their being **married**. Ariel now brings the ship's Master and **Boatswain** to the cell, unharmed. Caliban, **Stephano** and Trinculo are also driven in by Ariel and, while Alonso recognises Stephano and __**Trinculo**__, Prospero takes the responsibility for __**Caliban**__, who appears to have seen the error of his ways. Prospero __**releases**__ Ariel, asking him only to provide fair __**winds**__ for their return journey to __**Italy**__. In the epilogue, Prospero turns to the **audience** and asks them to set him free with their **applause**.

THE ENDING OF *THE TEMPEST*
TEACHERS' VERSION

Solution (page 25)

	The Tempest	*A Midsummer Night's Dream*	*All's Well That Ends Well*	*As You Like It*
Who delivers the Prologue?	*Prospero, the main character*	*Puck, a minor character of mischief*	*King, a minor character*	*Rosalind, the main character (and female)*
Is the actor in character?	*Debateable – at the beginning he seems to be in character; when addressing audience mixture of Prospero and actor*	*Yes, but aware that he is talking to an audience*	*No, he speaks as an actor who is no longer the king, but a "beggar"*	*No, philosophises about the structure of plays and the worth of epilogues*
How is the character trying to persuade the audience to clap?	*Imploring them to release him from island through the clapping as he has no more magic. Wind produced by hands will propel his sails*	*No persuasion, more argument: if the audience are dissatisfied, it was all a dream, if they are satisfied, they should clap*	*Title not true until audience claps; actors at mercy of audience*	*Appealing to men and women to persuade each other; the promise of a kiss from her*
How do you think the actor would deliver the speech – and what does that tell you about the character?	*Despairing at loss of magic, humble that he is dependent on others – more man than magician, no longer the controlling force*	*Softly at beginning, as if a dream, then more resolutely – cautious, but still cunning nature; roundabout arguments*	*Sincerely, humbly – even kings are nothing, need approval*	*Flippantly, mock-philosophising – women can be as good as men or better as they can charm more*

Solution (page 28)

FAMILY TREE
TEACHERS' VERSION

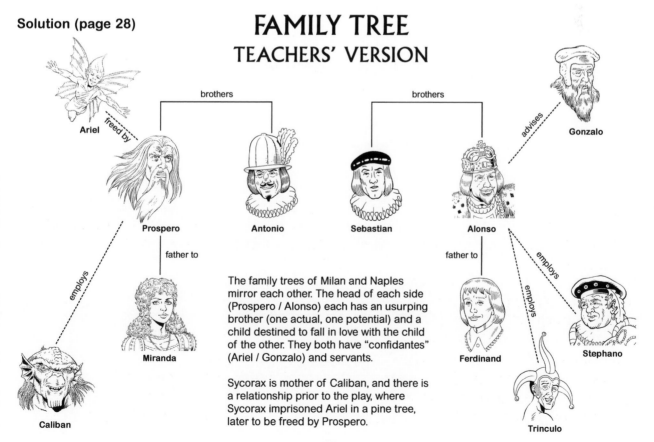

The family trees of Milan and Naples mirror each other. The head of each side (Prospero / Alonso) each has an usurping brother (one actual, one potential) and a child destined to fall in love with the child of the other. They both have "confidantes" (Ariel / Gonzalo) and servants.

Sycorax is mother of Caliban, and there is a relationship prior to the play, where Sycorax imprisoned Ariel in a pine tree, later to be freed by Prospero.

FERDINAND'S LABOURS
TEACHERS' VERSION

Solution (page 52)

Answers are in bold below.

There be some <u>sports</u> are <u>painful</u>, and their ***labour***

Delight in them sets off: some kinds of <u>baseness</u>

Are ***nobly*** undergone, and most <u>poor</u> matters

Point to ***rich*** ends. This my mean task

Would be as heavy to me as odious, but

The mistress which I serve <u>quickens</u> what's ***dead,***

And makes my <u>labours</u> ***pleasures***; O, she is

Ten times more <u>gentle</u> than her father's crabbed,

And he's compos'd of ***harshness***. I must remove

Some thousands of these logs, and pile them up,

Upon a <u>sore</u> injunction: my ***sweet*** mistress

Weeps when she sees me work; and says, such baseness

Had never like executor.

Word	Its opposite
sports	**labour**
painful	**delight**
baseness	**nobly**
poor	**rich**
quickens	**dead**
labours	**pleasures**
gentle	**harshness**
sore	**sweet**

INSULTING PROSPERO AND CALIBAN
TEACHERS' VERSION

Solution (page 55)

Answers are in bold below.

Prospero vs Caliban	Caliban vs Prospero
slave	**as wicked dew as e'er my mother brush'd... from unwholesome fen, drop on you both!**
tortoise	**a southwest blow on ye, and blister you all o'er!**
poisonous slave, got by the devil himself upon thy wicked dam	**all the charms of Sycorax, toads, beetles, bats, light on you!**
most lying slave	**the red plague rid you**
filth as thou art	**all the infections that the sun sucks up ... on Prosper fall, and make him by inch-meal a disease! (thought, or spoken behind Prospero's back)**
Here are a few more suggestions	
hag-seed	
malice	
misshapen knave	
demi-devil	
bastard one	
thing of darkness	

EXPLORING THEMES
TEACHERS' VERSION

Solution (page 57)

(Act I Scene I and Act I Scene II, lines 1-32)

Themes	Evidence from the text	Explain relevance of evidence
justice & fate	Storm as "vengeance from above"? Gonzalo believes Boatswain's "complexion is pure gallows".	While Prospero calls up the storm he could not control the passing of the ship – fate put the ship in his hands, and he makes the most of it. Only what is destined to happen will happen. In the play, Prospero almost takes over the role of fate.
magic	Storm brewed by magic. Miranda wishes she were a "God of power" in order to help those perishing in the storm.	Chain of events of the play set in motion by magic, just as Prospero will control all subsequent events by magic. Shows him, God-like, in control of plot and characters. The play is, arguably, about Prospero's return to humanity.
colonisation	Although we only learn this later, the ship is returning from the marriage of King of Naples' daughter to King of Tunis – a form of colonial venture, securing the influence of Europe in Africa.	Ship was coming back from a "colonial" enterprise, European royalty trying to assert influence in Africa.
legitimate rule & social order	Boatswain orders courtiers (socially his superiors) below deck and is rude to them: "what cares these roarers for the name of king?" The storm wrecks the "royal" ship of state.	Seems to turn around accepted social order, but on the ship he is the legitimate ruler, in a way that the courtiers never are (being all usurpers in the widest sense). Idea of legitimate ruler guiding ship of state through storm (but there is no legitimate/blameless ruler, so the ship founders).
	Possible extra themes	
loyalty	The courtiers appear loyal to the King ANTONIO: Let's all sink wi' th' king. SEBASTIAN: Let's take leave of him.	In their darkest hour, before imminent death, the courtiers show their loyalty to the King. Of course, we soon learn how this is a shallow offering – both Sebastian and Antonio are ambitious and show no loyalty.
fate	Prospero is fatalistic about arriving at the island. After all, it allowed him to perfect his magic and control spirits, including Ariel. "By foul play, as thou say'st, were we heav'd thence; But blessedly holp thither." Fate also brought his enemies near to the same island: "By accident most strange, bountiful Fortune, Now my dear lady, hath mine enemies Brought to this shore;"	Prospero has managed to turn around the foul play into good fortune. All he wanted to do while in Milan was to perfect his learning and magic, and landing upon the island has allowed him to do just that – and to a level that would have been impossible in Milan. He has prepared himself, and now fate has presented the opportunity for him to exact his revenge.

BETRAYAL AND FORGIVENESS
TEACHERS' VERSION

Solution (page 58)

Characters	How?	What was their motive for betrayal?	Are they forgiven?	Do they regret their actions?
Prospero betrays Ariel	By delaying his freedom (Act I, Sc II, 242-249)	Because he needed Ariel to carry out his demands	Yes	No
Alonso betrayed Prospero	Helped Antonio to become duke by forcing Prospero out of Milan and casting him out to sea (Act I Sc II, 108-132)	The King could effectively control Antonio, and so he could control Milan. Also, he charged higher taxes	Yes	Yes
Sebastian tries to betray Alonso	Is easily convinced to kill his brother, King Alonso (Act II, Sc I, 205-294)	Ambition to become King himself	No, because the king never knew	No evidence of regret
Antonio betrayed Prospero	Arranged for Prospero to be sent away (killed) (Act I Sc II, 108-132)	He wanted to be Duke of Milan and to have power	Yes	No evidence of regret
Antonio tries to betray Alonso	Convinces Sebastian to become King and threatens to kill Alonso (Act II, Sc I, 205-294)	To help his friend to become King and therefore ease the burden that Alonso has placed upon him	Yes	No evidence of regret
Gonzalo betrayed Alonso	By helping Prospero with provisions when he was sent from Milan (Act I, Sc II, 159-168)	A desire to be humane and to show some friendship / loyalty to Prospero	No, because the king never knew	No
Caliban betrays Prospero	Joining forces with Stephano and Trinculo, plotting to kill Prospero (Act III, Sc II, 87-105)	To release himself from slavery under Prospero	No evidence of forgiveness, but also none of punishment	Yes

COLONISATION AND ACQUIRING LAND
TEACHERS' VERSION
Solution (page 60)

Question	Answer	Relevance to *The Tempest*
Was Bermuda inhabited before the English arrived or did another country have a claim to priority?	Not permanently. It was discovered by the Spanish; due to its reputation and the frequent storms, no colony was established; although there were plans to use it as a re-filling station (by releasing pigs). There was a possible Portuguese claim to priority (stranded sailors lived there for four months).	Whether the island was inhabited before Sycorax arrived is not known. How she took control of the island is also unknown. Caliban seems to have lived there on his own for at least 12 years, making him the owner. His loss of the island reflects colonisation, in that a greater power just takes the land it wants.
What methods are there generally for claiming "new" land?	Taking by force, which negates any claim of natives to the land. Negotiating for the use (or ownership) of land with natives (who might not be interested in that land) – this avoids the issue of ownership. Buying land from the natives (and thus recognising that they owned it, prior to purchase).	It seems that originally Prospero might have been willing to share the island with Caliban (so second alternative), thus avoiding any questions of ownership. After Caliban's attempted rape of Miranda, Prospero enslaved Caliban and thus effectively took over the island, making it his colony. Of the courtiers, only Gonzalo entertains any ideas of claiming the island (cf next question).
What is the basis for claiming land in a colony?	Once land has been claimed for a country or monarch, individuals or companies are given the right (derived from the monarch) to grant property rights in the new colony. Behind this is the power of the monarch, represented through army and navy.	Gonzalo, in his vision, seems to imply that a charter would be required to take ownership of the island. This suggests that the island has in some way been claimed – presumably through the landing of his king there.
In what way – if at all – were the natives given any form of compensation?	If land was taken by violence, no compensation was given. Later on, land was bought from natives, but usually at a very low rate, not an adequate compensation.	Caliban (or former inhabitants before Sycorax) received no compensation; on the contrary, it is Caliban who gives up the "treasures" of the island. In a role reversal, Caliban then seeks some form of compensation by persuading Stephano to kill Prospero.

THE COLONISATION OF THE ISLAND
TEACHERS' VERSION

Solution (page 62)

Explanation (based on Act I Scene II):

Stephano is of course last – he never actually takes control of the island; his "kingship" is in an implausible future that is never realised in the play.

Before him comes Prospero, as the only arrival on the island that we know of before the courtiers and the beginning of the play, and after Sycorax. Between Sycorax's death and Prospero's arrival, the island belonged to Caliban.

It seems that Ariel was on the island before Sycorax arrived, because he knows the island was unpopulated before Caliban was born (lines 283-286). Prospero says that Ariel was Sycorax's servant when she was left on the island (the "then" in lines 273 is ambiguous and could mean "later" or "at that time"), but it makes more sense to assume Ariel was on the island beforehand, rather than that he had been Sycorax's slave before then, because this begs the question why he did not rebel before he arrived on the island. The end of the play shows that Ariel is not, however, a spirit of the island. This means there is likely to have been someone on the island prior to him.

The question mark should therefore be at the beginning – we do not know who was on the island before Ariel. It could also be at the end, as we do not know what will happen after the play has ended. One could argue that Caliban will inherit the island when the Europeans head back to Milan. It is not clear whether he goes along with them, and therefore he could also be placed in last position as well as 4th.

THE SHIPWRECK ON BERMUDA
TEACHERS' VERSION

Solution (page 63)

Question	Answer
To what extent does the account of the storm match or differ from Shakespeare's description?	The *Sea Venture* was the flagship of a convoy, much like the ship in the play. The courtiers cry louder than the weather (the Reportory mentions the clamours drowning in the wind). In both reports the ships are touched by Elmo's fire. In the Reportory, all assist in keeping the ship afloat; in *The Tempest* the courtiers are told to keep off deck. When they think all is lost, they give themselves up to God or start praying; but in the Reportory they then see land – and they wreck the ship on purpose.
What names contained in Strachey's report crop up again in *The Tempest*? Why do you think this might be?	Bermuda. A famously stormy island, at the time believed to be inhabited by witches and demons, and it is the site of the wreck. Ariel mentions the Bermudas as the goal of one his errands in a sentence describing where he hid the ship. Algiers. This is where Sycorax hails from. Mentioned in the Reportory as a place in which Strachey had been in a storm (possibly when fighting the pirates there). Gonzalo. The Reportory mentions a Gonzalus Ferdinandus Orviedus, who wrote about the size and history of the West Indies and attempted to set Bermuda up as a "filling station" for Spanish ships.
To what extent is the description of Bermuda similar or different to the island?	Contrary to superstition (domain of witches and devils) Bermuda was "normal". The island in the play is full of musical spirits and was the abode of Sycorax, a witch. Caliban seems to be semi-human, allegedly begot of the devil. Bermuda has the sustenance to support life, including trees – this is implicit in the play, too (Caliban fetches wood). Bermuda has no rivers or running springs; Caliban shows Prospero and promises to show Stephano where the fresh springs are.
What do all these clues and parallels suggest about the setting and the theme of the play?	Due to the nature of reference to Bermuda, it is speculated that the play is set there. Colonialism and the taking of land are obviously important themes, as a shipwreck led to the English crown claiming Bermuda. Survivors wanted to stay on the island, as a sort of paradise, rather than go on to Virginia. In the play, Gonzalo muses on the ideal form of state with him as administrator.

ALCOHOL AND COLONISATION
TEACHERS' VERSION

Solution (page 64)

Question	Answer	Relevance to *The Tempest*
Did the natives know about alcohol before the arrival of the settlers?	It seems they did have certain forms of alcohol, but certainly not the range the Europeans did. Alcohol also seems to have been more controlled in distribution before the arrival of the European settlers.	Caliban, it seems, does not know about alcohol. This may reflect the common belief at the time (that the Indians did not have alcohol), but Shakespeare may have consciously changed facts to show the depravity of the courtiers as opposed to the "innocent" native.
What was alcohol primarily used for by the natives?	Like most other drugs, alcohol was mainly used for religious purposes, as a means of communicating with the Gods during trance. As such, it would be regulated and probably not freely available.	Caliban calls the alcohol "celestial liquor" and therefore assumes that whoever bears it must be a god.
Was alcohol used purposefully by the settlers?	Allegedly the settlers used alcohol to make the natives more tractable and to make negotiations with them easier. This is still done by Russians today.	Stephano originally gives Caliban the wine to cure him of ague, but as he realises the effect the alcohol has on Caliban, Stephano seems to use it to make Caliban more malleable.
In what way was alcohol detrimental to the natives?	Widespread alcoholism had repercussions on social life and employability. Alcohol led to the break-up of traditional communities and to crime in order to obtain further supply of alcohol.	Caliban, under the influence of alcohol, swears allegiance to Stephano and promises to serve him faithfully. However, it is he who tries to use Stephano for his own ends, rather than the other way round.

MAGICIAN AND BARD
TEACHERS' VERSION

Solution (page 72)

Action	How does this apply to Prospero?	How does this relate to Shakespeare?
Watching action from off-stage	When Miranda and Ferdinand declare their love (Act III Scene I) Banquet scene (Act III Scene III) Caliban, Trinculo and Stephano come to murder Prospero and are distracted by finery (Act IV Scene I)	As playwright (and actor), Shakespeare would watch his plays during rehearsals and actual performances to make sure everything was just as he wanted it to be.
Setting up other characters for "scenes"	Making Ferdinand work for him (Act III Scene I) Putting out the finery for Caliban et al to find (Act IV Scene I) Revealing Ferdinand and Miranda playing chess (Act V Scene I)	Shakespeare's plays reflect, to some degree, his personality and what he considered to be important – thus he sets scenes for the audience to develop and learn, much like Prospero does in the play.
Conjuring up strange worlds	The banquet (Act III Scene III) and the masque (Act IV Scene I); to a certain degree the tempest itself (Act I Scene I) and the strange sights and sounds of the island	Writing plays is obviously recreating different worlds (cf. Prospero's speech in Act IV Scene I) partly for entertainment purposes, partly for didactic reasons.
Being involved in the action he devises	As principal character, Prospero is of course involved in the play, but the desired end results of his schemes are his reinstatement as Duke of Milan and the securing of his succession with the marriage of Ferdinand and Miranda (Naples and Milan) – events in which he himself is involved.	Shakespeare was an actor as well as a playwright and therefore would have performed a great number of his roles. When writing, he was possibly imagining himself acting the part.
Staging plays	Prospero stages the masque (Act IV Scene I), the tempest (Act I Scene I) and the banquet (Act III Scene III). To a lesser degree he also stages the discovery of Miranda and Ferdinand and the revelation of himself as Duke of Milan (both Act V Scene I).	As well as writing the plays, Shakespeare also staged them. Although meant to entertain, much like the masque, he uses them to deliver his messages about human nature and topical happenings.

SLAVERY AND SERVITUDE
TEACHERS' VERSION

Solution (page 73)

Prospero talks in a kindly manner to Ariel but reminds him who is in charge to keep him in line. On the other hand, he talks harshly to Caliban, and from what he says in Act II Sc II, torments him. In return, Caliban talks harshly to Prospero, and surprisingly Prospero doesn't reprimand or punish Caliban for doing so.

If Caliban found out about Ariel, he would probably be sullen, knowing that he now has more than one powerful master. He might even try to convince Ariel to kill Prospero, much like he did with Stephano.

THE TEMPEST WORD SEARCH
TEACHERS' VERSION

Solution (page 93)

SEBASTIAN	MILAN	NAPLES
PROSPERO	SPIRIT	GONZALO
KING	DUKE	FERDINAND
SERVANT	SETEBOS	BERMUDA
MIRANDA	TRINCULO	ARIEL
DIDO	ALGIERS	FRANCISCO
BOATSWAIN	CALIBAN	TUNIS

THE TEMPEST WORD SEARCH
TEACHERS' VERSION

Solution (page 94)

LIQUOR	(5)	TREACHEROUS	(2)	GARMENT	(1)	VENGEANCE	(5)
PREROGATIVE	(5)	APPARITION	(1)	PLANTATION	(4)	CONFIDENCE	(4)
INVETERATE	(1)	MARKETABLE	(1)	AFFLICTION	(5)	GRUMBLINGS	(2)
VILLAINOUS	(2)	INSUBSTANTIAL	(3)	FATHOMS	(1)	USURP	(4)
IMPOSTER	(2)	DESTINY	(4)	THUNDERCLAPS	(1)	DILIGENCE	(1)
LANGUAGE	(3)	HARPY	(7)	BETRAYAL	(1)	PERFIDIOUS	(4)

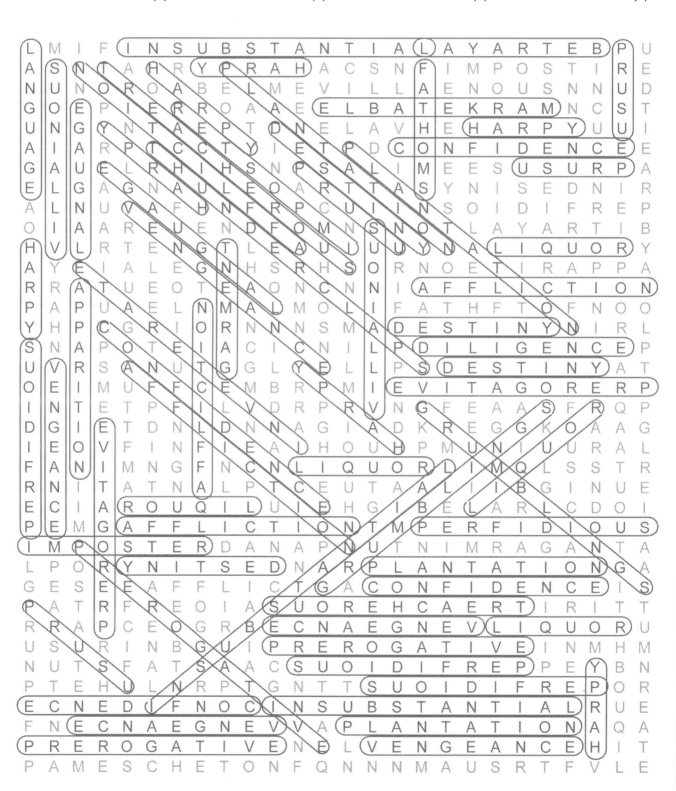

110

WHO AM I?
TEACHERS' VERSION

Solution (page 95)

Alonso

Antonio

Ariel

Caliban

Ferdinand

Prospero

Miranda

Gonzalo

The crossword solution:

```
        C A L I B A N
        R       B           S
  T     I       O           T
P R O S P E R O A       F   E       G
  I     L       A       E   P       O
  N   A L O N S O       R   H       N
  C             W       D   A       Z
  U     S E B A S T I A N   N   A N T O N I O
  L     Y       I       N   O       Z
  O     C       N       A           A
        O           A N T O N I O    L
  M I R A N D A     D                O
        R
        A
        X
```

Sebastian

Stephano

Trinculo

Sycorax

ACROSS

1 I was born on the island (7)
6 Before I was ousted, I used to be Duke of Milan (8)
9 I'm the King of Naples (6)
10 My brother is the King of Naples (9)
11 I ousted my brother to become Duke of Milan (7)
12 I grew up on the island and was taught by my father, who has magical powers (7)

DOWN

2 I am an airy spirit (5)
3 I am a jester to the King of Naples (8)
4 I tell the King and his courtiers to get below deck during the storm (9)
5 I am a butler to the King of Naples (8)
7 My father is King of Naples (9)
8 I am an advisor to the King of Naples (7)
10 I am a witch who gave birth on the island (7)

EDUCATIONAL WEBSITE LINKS

Listed below are a number of useful homepages for researching the colonisation of North America, in particular in relation to *The Tempest*. Remember when researching the web beyond these links to not spend too much time on search engines. Very often a book can provide a speedier, more age-adequate and more satisfactory answer!

Free scheme of work downloads
www.classicalcomics.com/tempest/schemeofwork

General Information
http://tinyurl.com/p8a5cn
http://tinyurl.com/yk6ds2z

Alcohol and Colonisation
www.answers.com/topic/indians-and-alcohol
www.authentichistory.com/diversity/native/alcohol/
www.essortment.com/all/nativeamerican_ragq.htm

The Shipwreck On Bermuda
http://tinyurl.com/lyhpul/
http://tinyurl.com/la59x6

Colonisation and Acquiring Land
www.directlinesoftware.com/landacq.htm
http://users.arn.net/~billco/uslpr.htm

Witchcraft
http://tinyurl.com/yfa7mp8
www.elizabethan-era.org.uk/elizabethan-witchcraft-and-witches.htm
http://tinyurl.com/ykx3ggw

Discoveries
www.elizabethan-era.org.uk/elizabethan-explorers-timeline.htm
www.royal-navy.org/lib/index.php?title=Elizabethan_Period

The Succession to the English Throne
www.historylearningsite.co.uk/elizabeth_succession.htm
www.history.ac.uk/ihr/Focus/Elizabeth/
www.elizabethan-era.org.uk/death-of-queen-elizabeth-i.htm

Elizabethan and Jacobean Theatre
www.elizabethan-era.org.uk/elizabethan-theatre.htm
http://members.fortunecity.com/fabianvillegas2/drama/jacobean.htm
www2.warwick.ac.uk/fac/arts/ren/elizabethan_jacobean_drama/